RUN TOWARD YOUR
GOLIATHS

Fighting with Faith to Overcome the Giants That Stop Your Personal and Professional Success

"In his book, *Run Toward Your Goliaths*, Dr. Eli Jones shares the compelling, challenging, and heartbreaking stories that are woven throughout the fabric of his life. One might think in looking at Eli's life today that he has had an easy road, getting lucky breaks along the way. But nothing could be further from the truth. He is intelligent, articulate, determined, and faithful to his Lord, family, and friends. In this book, you will find the source of Eli's success, which is accompanied by hard work, ingenuity, and sacrifice. Not only do his words challenge the reader to not sit idly while life passes one by, he inspires those on life's journey to cherish and appreciate those who mentor and mold us into who we are. Eli is living out his thesis by continuing to run toward the Goliaths in his life. Allow this book to help you identify the 'smooth stones' in your life as you will most certainly face giants of your own."

—**MICKEY RAPIER**, Fellowship Bible Church, Arkansas

"Tall, intimidating, and loud ... the giants of discouragement and challenge seek to loom in our lives. Yet with a skilled sling, a few stones, and the power of faith ... they can fall and fall hard. *Run Toward Your Goliaths* is a transparent testimony and training for us on how to take down the giants hindering our lives' forward progress. Dr. Jones will brilliantly lead you through his personal and heartfelt journey to the places of wisdom and victory God has for you!"

—**GREGG MATTE**, Pastor of Houston's First Baptist Church

"I've always said, in everything look for the good. We all face 'giants' in our lives and can feel defeated at times. But God is in all things, everywhere, at the same time, even when it may not feel like it. Look for the good! In *Run Toward Your Goliaths*, Eli Jones *takes you there*. He shares his testimonies about rising up and fighting with faith in times of trouble. On the other side of those spiritual battles, you will find miracles and God waiting to embrace you with His peace which surpasses all understanding."

—**AL BELL**, Former Chairman & Owner, Stax Records
Former President, Motown Records Group
Chairman and Chief Executive Officer, Al Bell Presents, LLC
Songwriter, "I'll Take You There"

RUN TOWARD YOUR GOLIATHS

Fighting with Faith to Overcome the Giants That Stop Your Personal and Professional Success

ELI JONES

HIGH BRIDGE BOOKS
HOUSTON

Run Toward Your Goliaths
by Eli Jones

Copyright © 2021 by Eli Jones
All rights reserved.

Printed in the United States of America
ISBN: 978-1-954943-23-0

All rights reserved. Except in the case of brief quotations embodied in critical articles and reviews, no portion of this book may be reproduced, stored in a retrieval system, or transmitted in any form or by any means—electronic, mechanical, photocopy, recording, scanning, or other—without prior written permission from the author.

Scripture quotations marked AMP are taken from the Amplified® Bible (AMP), Copyright © 2015 by The Lockman Foundation. Used by permission. www.lockman.org

Scripture quotations marked ESV are taken from The ESV® Bible (The Holy Bible, English Standard Version®), copyright © 2001 by Crossway, a publishing ministry of Good News Publishers. Used by permission. All rights reserved.

Scripture quotations marked NIV are taken from THE HOLY BIBLE, NEW INTERNATIONAL VERSION®, NIV® Copyright © 1973, 1978, 1984, 2011 by Biblica, Inc.® Used by permission. All rights reserved worldwide.

Scripture quotations marked NKJV are taken from the New King James Version®. Copyright © 1982 by Thomas Nelson. Used by permission. All rights reserved.

Scripture quotations marked NLT are taken from the Holy Bible, New Living Translation, copyright © 1996, 2004, 2015 by Tyndale House Foundation. Used by permission of Tyndale House Publishers, Inc., Carol Stream, Illinois 60188. All rights reserved.

High Bridge Books titles may be purchased in bulk for educational, business, fundraising, or sales promotional use. For information, please contact High Bridge Books via www.HighBridgeBooks.com/contact.

Published in Houston, Texas by High Bridge Books

CONTENTS

FOREWORD _____ IX

PROLOGUE _____ XIII

INTRODUCTION _____ XV

SECTION 1. BUILD ON YOUR FOUNDATION _____ 1

   1. Full Circle _____ 3

   2. Life Lessons from Dad _____ 15

   3. The Women in My Life: My Five Smooth Stones ____ 33

SECTION 2. FIND YOUR RHYTHM _____ 49

   4. The Drumbeat of Life _____ 51

   5. Discover Your Calling _____ 63

   6. The Discovery Process _____ 73

   7. The Road to the Ph.D. _____ 87

SECTION 3. DARE TO BELIEVE _____ 101

   8. Anchor and Float _____ 103

   9. The Academic Entrepreneur _____ 117

   10. A Custom-Made Suit … to Run in _____ 133

   11. God's Stretching Process _____ 147

   12. A Giant Step of Obedience _____ 165

13. Going Home _____ 185

14. Conclusion: Leaving a Legacy _____ 203

ACKNOWLEDGMENTS_____ 215

FOREWORD

Rare is the moment when a book emerges offering significantly more than printed words on a page. You are reading such a work right now. The thoughts, reflections, and experiences of renowned educator and gifted author Dr. Eli Jones combine to weave a tapestry displaying both a blueprint for overcoming adversity and a heavenly lifeline connecting us to the power of God. The poetic fusion offers a divinely robust strategy to defeat every giant in our lives.

Holy Scripture states, "If the foundations are destroyed, what can the righteous do?" (Ps. 11:3 ESV). For Eli and his siblings, the foundation was rock solid, and they needed to search no further than Godly parents and grandparents. Mr. and Mrs. Jones—building on the wisdom of their parents—taught largely by example. And righteousness indeed emerged as Godly principles married common sense to create a formidable bond that produced multiple successful businesses, college-educated children, and a lifetime of wisdom.

Greatness has no color, education level, or social standing. Greatness is remaining true to your values, using what you must to get what you need, never losing sight of your purpose, and determining that quitting is not an option. Without greatness in his DNA, Eli would have quit a time or two. He had every reason to quit. However, when the foundation is laid by architects who choose excellence over excuses, a demand is placed upon future generations to trust in the Lord and learn and execute tactics of spiritual warfare while being the best version of themselves. Each foundational brick demanded greater commitment and excellence from the new generation of Joneses to ensure that they, too, would continue the legacy of overcoming life's challenges.

With the precision of a surgeon and the pen of a poet, Eli simply and skillfully reconstructs the parental foundation, mining nuggets of wisdom and applying them to his life. I was struck by how often similar circumstances produced similar responses. For example, in his cleaning business, Mr. Jones would work on "one spot at a time" until a garment was clean. In one low-paying, entry-level job, Eli sold "one ad at a time" to get out of debt. It wasn't about status, prestige, or position but something far more important: the honor associated with doing your best. The integrity earned when you keep your word. The character developed when you choose not to quit. From the "sound of determination" to the profoundly strategic intention of "putting a pencil to it," we are left astonishingly spellbound by simple common sense wisdom. The type of wisdom that produces entrepreneurs. The type of wisdom that demands your best. The type of wisdom that compels one to "run toward your Goliaths!"

What I love most about this manuscript is its heart. As we read about adversity and tough times and even the death of loved ones, the words come alive, all the while reminding us that, like King David, we possess a divinely indomitable spirit to overcome. Through it all, Eli guides the reader with biblical wisdom based on that unshakable foundation.

Never in my lifetime have I sensed a greater urgency to read a book on overcoming the Goliaths in our lives. As the issue of mental health pushes from crisis to disaster, allow this book to encourage your soul and uplift your spirit. If you are struggling with abandonment, betrayal, disappointment, fear, intimidation, rejection, or self-pity, please read this book and apply its lessons to your life. The stories will captivate your heart; the wisdom will demand a change in your thinking. Along this literary journey, you will become convinced of the power of five smooth stones... and how we are designed by God to be overcomers.

FOREWORD

As a pastor, I've preached about defeating giants for decades. However, this book demands examining the ancient story from a modern lens. There is a tremendous application here that we can utilize every day as masterfully told stories dare us to run toward the giants in our lives.

If faith is the hallmark of our Christian heritage, defeating giants is the evidence of that faith, for according to the Bible, faith without works is dead. Eli Jones compels us to *do* something! To *try* something! To *imagine* something! It's the stuff of entrepreneurs who've built a solid foundation.

In a world where we'd rather be entertained than challenged, it's good to know there are still a few authors around who demand that we dream, have faith, fight, and overcome. I can see Mama Jones smiling and hear Daddy Jones whistling in heaven as they witness the foundation become even greater!

—**Rick Rigsby, Ph.D.**
President, Rick Rigsby Communications
Motivational Speaker, Minister, and Best-Selling Author,
Lessons From a Third-Grade Dropout

PROLOGUE

Run Toward Your Goliaths is about defeating various "giants" that one faces in a lifetime, such as coping with Death, overcoming Anxiety, Fear, Disappointment, Rejection, and persevering despite being Underestimated. As David faced Goliath with faith and the boldness of God's favor, I share scriptures and personal testimonies to help others conquer their giants.

We all face setbacks and disappointments in life. How we respond to these challenges makes the difference in overcoming them. For some time, I wanted to write a book directed solely to my family so that my children, grandchildren, and great-grandchildren to come would have the important history of who they are and whose they are; I was further prompted to write this book after the death of my eldest daughter during the summer of 2019. She left us with three beautiful grandchildren, and my wife and I stepped in to help fill the void. We are facing this giant by working through it together, praying, and remembering the happy times we had with her.

We received many books from friends about coping with the death of loved ones, but I decided to write a book about not only leaning on God while grieving the loss of loved ones but leaning on God while facing many *other* giants as well. I'm sharing the book that I originally intended for just my family with you, because several readers of early draft chapters suggested that others, too, may benefit from reading it.

This book has fourteen chapters, and each chapter takes the average reader fifteen to twenty minutes to read. Reviewers who have read drafts of the chapters have described the book as "authentic" and "inspiring."

THOUGHTS ABOUT HOW TO USE THE BOOK

This book is a collection of personal testimonies with scriptures that I found helpful when going through challenging times. Included are stories of how God has turned dark moments into sheer miracles. It's organized into four sections: (1) Build on Your Foundation, (2) Find Your Rhythm, (3) Dare to Believe, and (4) Leave a Legacy.

Each chapter opens with a thought-starter to set the tone for the chapter and to get you to reflect. I encourage you to pause at the beginning of each chapter and think about the thought-starter posed before reading on.

At the end of each chapter, there is a summary that highlights key points of the chapter, titled "Five Smooth Stones." Some of the stones are questions to get you to reflect more on what the chapter inspires you to do or think, and some stones are statements for you to consider.

Another thing that makes this book different is I include song lyrics from my wife's work as a vocalist, songwriter, and performer. The song lyrics are placed in the book to reinforce the key points about the stories that we share and to make those stories more memorable.

We pray that this book inspires and encourages you and that God touches you in very special ways as you read *Run Toward Your Goliaths*.

INTRODUCTION

As the Philistine moved closer to attack him, David ran quickly toward the battle line to meet him.

—1 Samuel 17:48 NIV

In the Bible, the book of 1 Samuel tells of a giant Philistine warrior named Goliath. The man stood over nine feet tall and wore armor weighing over 100 pounds. He carried a spear that had a sharp iron point weighing about fifteen pounds. This was indeed a giant of a man. Battles were a sport for him. He was born and bred for one purpose: to fight and win.

Now in those days, the Philistines were arrayed in battle against King Saul's Israelite army. But instead of whole troops charging at one another in combat, Goliath came forward and proposed an alternative. "Choose a man and have him come down and fight me. If he is able to kill me, we will become your subjects; but if I overcome him and kill him, you will become our subjects and serve us. I defy the armies of Israel! Give me a man, and let us fight each other." But there was no Israelite soldier brave enough to take him on. Not even King Saul, a man who was said to be "head and shoulders above every man."

Jesse had three sons who were fighting in Saul's army. But Jesse's youngest son, David, thought too young for battle, stayed home tending to the sheep.

Jesse sent David to the battlefield to deliver some food and bring home news from the frontline. But when David arrived at the frontline, he was surprised to see no battle taking place, instead finding the Israelite army, including the king himself, cowering in fear and doing their best to block out the giant's taunts.

David didn't know warfare, but he knew the God of Abraham, Isaac, and Jacob. He'd grown up listening to stories about the exploits of men like Moses and mighty warriors like Joshua and Caleb. David was mystified as to why God's army was hiding in their tents instead of engaging this blowhard. In David's view, he'd killed both lions and bears with his sling and a well-aimed stone while watching over his father's sheep. He told the king, "The Lord who rescued me from the paw of the lion and the paw of the bear will rescue me from the hand of this Philistine."

David rejected the king's armor, choosing to enter the fray in his own clothes. Then, armed with just his trusty sling, he made his way down to a small stream running along the floor of the valley, where he quickly selected **five smooth stones** and put them in his shepherd's bag. As David came out to meet the giant, Goliath mocked him, calling David a dog, laughing at David's weakness: his lack of weaponry or armor.

But David was undeterred. "You come to me with your sword and spear, but I come against you with much more than a simple sling and stone. I come against you with the name of the Lord. Today, my God will deliver you into my hands. I'll strike you down and cut off your head!"

David didn't cower or cringe. He didn't retreat or back down. Instead, he pulled his shoulders back and *ran toward the battle line to meet Goliath.*

David defeated Goliath with his sling and a stone. He cut off the giant's head, held it up, and declared victory in the name of the Lord. Now that the giant was dead, the Israelite army was filled with boldness, and they pursued the Philistines, slaying every one of them.

INTRODUCTION

FACING GOLIATH

I love the story of David. Growing up Catholic and attending Catholic school, I've been familiar with the story of David and the giant Goliath since I was a young man. Captured by the tale, I identified with David, the shepherd boy, and I could easily imagine myself in his place, armed with just a simple slingshot, charging into battle against insurmountable odds. But, as I grew up into a mature adult, the story lost some of its appeal, its meaning, and some of its power.

Until one day, God brought the story back to my memory.

Like most everyone else, my days are busy, full of appointments and meetings, many unplanned. For me to have any time with the Lord, it must be early in the day, before the "busyness" begins. Over the years, I've found the best time to connect with God is during my morning shower. As I take the soap, I pray that the Lord would cover me with his blood of protection, inspiration, and love, just like the soapy lather, from my head down to my toes.

In this time of prayer, God will usually give me something to think about—a kind of "word for the day." While I was in prayer in the shower a while back, God gave me a different kind of word: a name. In my head, I heard the name "Goliath." I was used to hearing words like love, forgive, faith, or gratefulness, but this one, Goliath, caught me a little off guard.

I thought, *Goliath. Now that's interesting.* In a flash, the story from scripture came rushing back to my mind—the massive warrior, fearsome and prepared for battle, taunting the armies of the living God. And a shepherd boy, standing before him, small and vulnerable but defiant, *not even realizing he was supposed to be scared.*

That day, as I thought about this story with the fresh perspective of a grown man, the tale took on a whole new meaning for me. In this new light, it was easy to see how, in many ways, we're all like David. We all have giants in our lives, reminding

— xvii —

us of our sin, our weakness, opposing our purpose, taunting us, and daring us to act. When faced with these challenges, do we shrink back, or do we rise with courage like David and run toward the Goliaths in our lives?

RUN TOWARD YOUR GOLIATHS

Throughout each of our lives, we're all going to cross paths with Goliaths. Some will be unwarranted, unexpected, and heart-wrenching. Goliaths in our lives mock and taunt us. They're attracted by our fear, desperation, and past failures.

Today, our giants have different appearances, various weaponry, and tactics. They come at us using different strategies, but one thing is sure: they are all fearsome and formidable.

There's a giant called Fear and one called Disappointment. There's Worry that attacks us in many areas. But what about the giants of Rejection, Risk, Loss, Underestimation, Unrealized Expectations, Hurt, Confusion, Self-Image, or even Uncertainty, and Waiting? These can all be Goliaths in our lives as well.

I'll share with you stories from my life of facing giants and the life-altering lessons learned. Stories of a young married couple with children, going to school, working multiple jobs, trying to make ends meet—to levels of miraculous success and influence. This book is all about how my wife Fern and I faced the Goliaths that stood in our path, daring us to act. In our case, we met those giants with our faith in God and each other. We vowed to stick together no matter what. It was that commitment to overcome together that was key for us.

I'D LIVE IN A DITCH WITH YOU

Early on in my life, I was confronted by giants on every front. I had a young family, no job, and another child on the way. It was overwhelming. The giants in my life were ever-present, taunting

INTRODUCTION

me, mocking me every minute of every day. But Fern encouraged me, thank God! Her belief in me, coupled with her faith in God, was like stones in my shepherd's bag, giving me the strength and the courage to take on those giants.

Goliath, and a few of his buddies, came calling at one of the lowest points of my life. Giants are opportunists, often waiting until you're down before they attack. I had just left my only job, Fern was pregnant, and I didn't have a plan. I clung tightly to Fern and tried to encourage her with a confidence that I didn't really feel. We were broke, and I was scared. The giants of Fear, Failure, Poverty, and Dread were circling, beating me down with their accusations.

At the time, Fern and I and our small children stayed overnight in a small room at the Holiday Plaza Motel, a one-star motel on Texas Avenue in Bryan, Texas. I was facing some of the darkest hours of my life and was down on myself because I was without a job only months after graduating from Texas A&M University with a journalism degree. At ages twenty-three and twenty-one, Fern and I had a lot of responsibility weighing down on us, a couple of kids barely out of our teenage years. I was already feeling the pressure of being responsible for three children, and now Fern was pregnant with our fourth.

The room was rented for twenty-five dollars a night, and it was all we could afford. It felt like we had hit rock bottom. I was sweating profusely with worry over how I would provide for my family's future, much less pay for another baby on the way. With no job, no health insurance, and no nest egg in a bank account, I had no clue what I was going to do.

At that low moment, my beautiful bride had every right to complain, every right to be angry, and even every right to leave me. The giant hurled his massive spear at me, reminding me that I was a dismal failure as a man and head of the household. I felt that I had let down my family and disappointed my parents. It seemed that I was not the man I had hoped I'd be. I thought that I had completely failed.

Pacing the floor in desperation, I couldn't help but notice how Fern responded to the situation. She was laughing! Now, if you have ever met my beautiful wife, you know that her laugh is unforgettable. It is loud and joyful, and it changes the atmosphere of the room. She laughed and said, "Eli, I would live in a ditch with you, as long as we're together. God will take care of us. We will be okay!"

Wow! Live in a *ditch* with me? Her words showed her love and commitment to our marriage. "God will take care of us!" Her declaration underscored her faith in God and bolstered mine. Like David's smooth stone, her words silenced the giants' voices in my head. And Fern's laughter? It was an amazing gift, especially during a pivotal moment that would set the stage for how we would handle life's challenges for nearly forty years together.

Many years later, Fern wrote a song based on our "in a ditch" moment. She dedicated the song to me, and the lyrics touch my heart, even all these years later.

"In a Ditch"

I said I would live in a ditch with you that day in stormy weather
I knew there was nothing we couldn't do as long as we were together
Because I believed in you, I saw the courage you carried
And all you're willing to do, so I anchored, you floated
And God saw us through, and I'm so proud to see all that you have achieved

I said I'd live in a ditch with you. This love is without measure
We've come full circle and, one thing is true, we'll always be together

Because I believe in you, I know that you're just a man
But I see the Savior in you, so I anchor, you float and
I'm so proud to be a part of this amazing legacy

Oh, oh, baby!
So I would live in a ditch with you, always and forever
I will always run this race with you, honey
Because this journey is our testimony
Always, always, always, and forever

FACING GIANTS WITH THE BOLDNESS OF CHRIST

With the boldness of Christ and unshakable faith in God, we were able to face down those Goliaths that night in that motel room. And it's the way we still face the giants in our lives today. Together, we've learned to take the battle to the giants by running toward them, not empty-handed but full of the boldness that Christ gives us.

As you read this book, you may find yourself in a ditch, surrounded by giants, with no clue how to get out. You may be in a challenging time that has taken something out of you, perhaps leaving you feeling broken inside or considering giving up on your dreams. You may be facing any number of giants, an illness or grief from the loss of a relationship, a loved one, job, health, finances, or a dream. You may even be facing significant opposition—perhaps even undeserved—from loved ones. Or even worse, you may be carrying the shame of living with the consequences of your own decisions and actions. Regardless, this book is for you. It is my prayer, and Fern's too, that as you read stories about our struggles and victories through Christ, you would be encouraged. We pray God will reveal weapons you can use to fight and defeat the giants in your own life.

SECTION 1

BUILD ON YOUR FOUNDATION

1

FULL CIRCLE

Thought-starter: Is your life built on your circumstances or on your decisions?

FULL CIRCLE

If I were to say the words "full circle" to you, what image would pop into your mind? Most see a simple round shape bordered by a single line that ends back where it began. People have a way of viewing life that way. In their minds, they have a somewhat idealistic view of how life will go for them. When they imagine a circle, more times than not, it's perfect, with no defects.

But life is never like that. Real life is messy, at times inconsistent, and even chaotic. It's never that simple and rarely moves along a simple curved line, ending in the exact spot that it began. We all may strive for a life that resembles a perfect circle, with no surprises, no sudden unplanned turns, and no jerky starts or stops. We want a life of consistency, each day seamlessly flowing into the next. But that's not realistic.

All of us have endured lives full of twists and turns, and if we're honest, most of the twists and turns come upon us unexpectedly, unplanned. Let me show you another, much different version of what "full circle" can look like.

ANOTHER CIRCLE

I use this graphic a lot when I speak to groups. I'll put this image up on the screen and ask people to examine it closely and tell me what they see. Most of the time, they'll point out the twists and turns first. They notice that the line curves and swirls and doesn't move along a predictable arc.

People also tend to notice the dark spots, the places along the way where the line passes through shadows. They may comment on the bright spots as well, but they all see those ominous dark spots.

I'll challenge the audience to look deeper and tell me more about what they see. It may take a few minutes, but someone will eventually realize that they're looking at a circle. This one is definitely not pristine and perfect. It seems random and full of unexpected bends and curves. But I believe this diagram more closely resembles our lives, with all its imperfections and its many twists and turns along the way.

Life is never going to roll out in a perfectly linear way. Expect twists and turns. There will be dark spots, times when the line of your life passes through the shadows. What can you do to prepare for these twists and turns?

THE LIFE YOU NEVER EXPECTED

Let's face it; life is never going to roll out in a perfectly linear way. It's never going to be a perfect circle. There will always be parts with sharp turns—times when you imagined life would go one way, but it quickly turned in a different direction. You may have thought you were going to move through life along a relatively ordered and predictable path. Graduating from high school, going to college, getting a degree, getting married, starting a promising career, raising kids, and so on. In your mind, each step is carefully planned, measured, and expected.

But be honest, do you know anyone whose life has turned out perfectly, just as they planned? Probably not, and neither do I. Everyone's life has had twists and turns along the way. Even if you can't see it from your outside perspective, I'll bet if you looked more in-depth, you'd find that their life isn't nearly as perfect as it may seem. We've all had times when we've expected one thing and gotten another. That's just the way things work out for most of us.

What about those dark spots? What about those places where the line seems to pass through a shadow? I'm sure you've experienced times like that in your life, too—times when you felt like you were going along just fine, with no big worries, cares, or concerns, and then suddenly you're groping along in the dark, not sure about where your next step should be. It's like one conversation, phone call, text, or email has come along and changed your world. In that instant, you've gone from being confident and secure to being timid and unsure of yourself. Here's another possible Goliath!

When you're in a dark place like that, it's easy to imagine that's the end of the world. You think to yourself, *Well, this is it, there's nothing more, things will always be like this. My life is ruined.*

Unfortunately, that's the way our minds work, assuming that whatever is happening now will continue to be the way things will happen in the future. It's as if our minds automatically go to the worst-case scenario and then fixate on that. But understand, all we see are bits and pieces at a time; we never see the bigger picture. Our vision only reaches the horizon, and that's if we're lucky. We lack the ability to see beyond.

All we see are bits and pieces at a time; we never see the bigger picture. It's important to trust God with the dark spots. He sees the beginning from the end and the end from the beginning. Life on earth is just a speck in time when we consider eternity with God.

It's like the difference between a video and a photo. With a photograph, all you get is that snapshot in time, without context, with no knowledge of what happened in the moments before and after the picture was taken.

But a video is different. With video, you get the full picture. You see how one scene leads to another, then the next, and so on.

That's how God sees our lives. He sees the big picture. He sees the beginning from the end and the end from the beginning.

If you find your life in the dark shadows right now, be encouraged! God sees you. The shadows are never so dark that God has lost you or doesn't know where you are. Just keep going, keep putting one foot in front of the other, determined to keep daring to believe in God, and eventually, you'll emerge back into the light.

My own life looks more like this imperfect, chaotic circle than the perfect one we imagined earlier. The course of my life has been far from predictable or from following along a pre-planned, well-thought-out path. Along the way, there have been times when I imagined my life was going to go in a particular direction. But, as you read this book, you will see that my life has really been nothing but twists and turns, some unpredictable, with lots of Goliaths in my path. The one constant, however, is that I kept moving, walking by faith and trusting that the Lord is in control.

We are not products of our circumstances.
We are products of the decisions we make.

Forty years ago, I could have never imagined that I would be doing what I'm doing today. I never in a million years thought I would go from being a radio DJ to being the dean of a business school at a top-tier university. As I look back, I can see that although some amazing things have happened, there have also been lots of dark spots—lots of times when I didn't know where I was or what I should do. I didn't know if I was going to make it or not.

Throughout my life, there have been lots of unexpected twists and turns. Times when I assumed I was finally on a stable path, only to be surprised by a hard left turn or a sharp dip in the road that threw me for a loop. But I kept moving, working hard, believing in God, and striving to make the best decisions I could make.

THREE BAD DECISIONS AWAY!

> *I am not a product of my circumstances. I am a product of my decisions.*
>
> —Stephen R. Covey

Our choices are like building blocks in our lives. The life we're living today is simply the result of the decisions we've made in our past. Right decisions build healthy, successful lives. But bad decisions build unsteady, faulty lives, liable to collapse at any moment. We're all just three bad decisions away from poverty and failure. Only three bad decisions away!

I share this truth often with the young men and women that attend a ministry that I founded in 2019 called "Five Fold Leaders." This non-profit engages, educates, and empowers underserved young men and women of color on the principles of Christian leadership.

A while back, we had a decision-making session with some young men and shared with them that we are three bad decisions away from poverty. Good decision-making has been an invaluable ingredient in my story, the story of coming full circle. Making sound decisions has played a crucial role in defeating the many Goliaths that have risen up against me.

Faith without works is dead. Keep moving forward and believing in God. Walk by faith, not by sight. Stay alert to those who God sends to help you at each crossroads.

THE TWISTS AND TURNS OF MY LIFE

I've had the privilege of teaching around the world. I've gone to some incredible places, speaking to corporate executives in places like Dubai, France, the United Kingdom, China, and other locations worldwide. It's just incredible to imagine all this when thinking back on where I've come from. I was just a kid who grew up in Sunnyside's little community, just south of downtown Houston, and later in a small town near Texas A&M. Now I'm back in Bryan-College Station after having traveled all over the world teaching executives. It blows my mind.

My mom finished high school, and my dad had only a sixth-grade education. My sister Jo Ann, who had a significant impact on me, was the first in my family to graduate from college. We'll talk about that in much more detail later in the book.

Like my sister, I'm a first-gen college graduate. It was tough for me trying to navigate the enormous Texas A&M University campus. When I was going to college in the late 70s, there were only about 30,000 students. Today, enrollment is more than double than when I started as a student, with almost 70,000 students.

I hit campus with no idea what I was doing. I didn't know the dining hall from the library. There was no one to talk to about which field of study to major in. No one to talk to about a calculus problem I was having in class. No one in my immediate family could help me navigate the campus or assist with the topics that I was studying. But God was always faithful to put just the right people in my path to show me the way at just the right time. Today, by God's grace, I have earned three degrees from Texas A&M. It has been an amazing journey.

And it's gotten more amazing as I've gotten older. I remember the phone call when I was asked to come home to A&M and lead Mays Business School, which is amazing in itself. For six years, I led the business school from which I graduated—an incredible honor. There were faculty members in the business school who taught me, and I became their boss's boss's boss, which really is unbelievable.

It's a great TESTimony. I feel a little bit like the Bible character Joseph. Like him, I went from feeling trapped and desperate to being in a tremendous position of authority and leadership. Talk about a life with some crazy twists and turns!

STARTING WITH A STRONG FOUNDATION

Being a first-generation college student, I had to learn early on how to fight the Goliaths who were trying to take me down. Thankfully, there were people in my life who were there right when I needed them, people who helped show me the way. It's just so interesting how God miraculously puts people in my path to help. There have always been people who were right there at different points in my life, making such a difference. I had to stay alert to those whom God sent my way.

If you want to build any kind of structure, at least one with any integrity, you'll need a proper foundation. Without a solid foundation to build upon, your project is doomed to fail. This first section of chapters is all about building a strong and secure foundation. So, what is your foundation?

My dad and mom, others in my family, and various teachers, mentors, coaches, and pastors that God brought into my life at just the right time have served to be an essential foundation for me. I'm just so grateful for the generosity of God to bless me by bringing these key people into my life. I'll mention some of them later in this book.

Think about your life. What establishes your foundation? There are people or experiences from which you can build. Even negative experiences can be learning experiences.

But what if you feel as if you don't have a solid foundation? What do you do then? Where can you go, who can you turn to? Fern and I were blessed not to have come from broken homes. In our case, coming from strong families has given us a leg up. But what if you come from a broken home and you don't have any kind of family support in your life? What if the adults in your life failed to encourage and undergird you? What then? What if you have a cracked and faulty foundation, or worse, no foundation at all?

Here's an example of running toward your Goliath. In 2019, a group of us formed Five Fold Leaders, a ministry and Bible study that encourages its members and educates the youth about Christian leadership. A young man whose dad walked away from the family joined our group. His mom is still young and has three kids; one of them is health challenged.

Running toward Goliath is the key to a strong foundation.

The sixteen-year-old didn't take on the role of a victim and wallow in self-pity. He didn't allow his life circumstance to make him angry and bitter, lashing out at anyone who tried to help. Instead, he decided to run toward his Goliath! His giant is Fatherlessness, so he joined Five Fold Leaders and surrounded himself with father figures! God made a way for us to encourage him and be his "Mighty Men." We shared with him the concept of having a heavenly father and said, "Hey man, we've got your back!"

By joining this organization, this young man now has multiple "dads." The mentors and I stepped up and embraced him in his journey. He took a step of faith and said, "Okay, I'm going to join this prayer group, this Bible study," and we welcomed him in with open arms.

If you've never had a strong foundation, let me encourage you to make a good decision right now and run toward your Goliath. If you can do this, I believe God will put just the right people in your path to propel you forward. Pushing through dark spots of your life and running toward Goliath is the key to a strong foundation, enabling you to move successfully through the twists and turns of your circle of life.

FIVE SMOOTH STONES

Just before David ran toward Goliath, he did something very important. Do you remember what it was? He'd already determined that Saul's armor, sword, and shield just weren't going to be right for him. He needed a weapon that fit him better, one that he was accustomed to using. So, what did he do? He went to the stream and collected five smooth stones. Those stones were his weapon of choice, and ultimately it was a stone that brought Goliath down.

In each chapter of this book, I'll be telling the stories of life lessons I've learned along my journey. These lessons are like smooth stones, valuable weapons you should add to your bag, ready for you to pull out and use. At the end of each chapter, I've listed that chapter's five smooth stones.

1. Think about your life. What establishes your foundation? There are people or experiences from which you can build. Even negative experiences can be learning experiences.

2. Life is never going to roll out in a perfectly linear way. Expect twists and turns. There will be dark spots, times when the line of your life passes through the shadows. What can you do to prepare for these twists and turns?

3. All we see are bits and pieces at a time; we never see the bigger picture. It's important to trust God with the dark spots. He sees the beginning from the end and the end from the beginning. Life on earth is just a speck in time when we consider eternity with God.

4. Faith without works is dead. Keep moving forward and believing in God. Walk by faith, not by sight. Stay alert to those who God sends to help you at each crossroads.

5. We are not products of our circumstances. We are products of the decisions we make.

Now, let me tell you about the foundation of my life.

2

LIFE LESSONS FROM DAD

Life lessons are sometimes better "caught" than "taught."

Thought-starter: Can you remember a time when you learned a life lesson by simply observing someone without a word being said?

MY DAD, ONE OF THE CORNERSTONES OF MY FOUNDATION

Think about the number of people who have had a significant influence on your life. Take a moment and allow their faces to scroll up in your mind. These are the people who caused you to think differently and who shaped your core values. Usually, when I ask an audience how many people are on their lists, the response is eye-opening. Most people will say there are just five or fewer influencers on their lists. When I ask who is at the top of their short lists, they'll tell me about an elementary or middle school teacher who said something or did something impactful that transformed their lives. Who's at the top of my list? It's simple: My dad is the one who tops my short list.

While in college, I had been working as a radio DJ in Houston, commuting 107 miles each way every weekend during my junior and senior years. After graduating from Texas A&M University in December of 1982 with my bachelor's degree, Fern and I married and moved from Houston to Bryan, Texas. Together with our children, we lived in a mobile home next to Jones Food Mart, my mom and dad's convenience store. After getting married, I went back to work for the first boss, mentor, and role model I ever had: my dad.

We all have influential people in our lives, and my father, Eli Jones, Jr., is still the most influential person in my life. Born in Sulphur, Louisiana, he was the fourth of five brothers. He joined the Army at an early age and picked up a trade—cleaning uniforms. After marrying my mom, Elvira Foote, who was born in Port Arthur, Texas, they had my two sisters, Elaine and Jo Ann. I was the third of four children. My brother Kirk came three and a half years after me. Our father had the most incredible impact on all of us. He was a wise man far ahead of his time.

In truth, we all stand on the shoulders of those who have gone before us and sacrificed so much on our behalf. Without a doubt, I stand on the shoulders of my father; most of the life lessons I've learned in life came from him. Born on July 11, 1921, he was the son of Eli Jones, Sr., and Della Mae Murphy Jones. My dad grew up on a ranch without a mother and had four brothers: Elward Jones, Howard Jones, Seward Jones, and Leonard T. Jones. (It's always intrigued me that my granddad named my dad after him, even though he was not the oldest, but rather the fourth of five sons. I'm honored to be Eli Jones III.) My dad later served our country in the United States Army during World War II.

Dad did not have an opportunity to finish high school, but he and my mom valued education and did everything they could to push us in that direction. When his youngest brother, Leonard, was born, his mom died tragically in childbirth. After a time, my grandfather remarried a schoolteacher from another town who came to my grandfather's farm to home-school my father and his siblings.

I believe that in his zeal to do better, my dad overcame the struggle of not having a mother. This teacher/stepmother really made an impact on my father. I believe it was she who whet my father's thirst for learning, a longing that remained unquenched for the rest of his life. Even though he only finished sixth grade, he continually impressed upon us the importance of getting an education. He always talked about how his stepmom read the Bible to him and his brothers every day. She was clearly near the top of my dad's list of influencers.

My father grew up somewhat of a rebel and moved away from his family in Louisiana at a young age. He always explained the move by telling us that he wanted to find a "better environment."

On May 29, 1947, he married my dear mama Elvira Foote, and together they created a strong legacy for our family. They did everything together. My dad honored my mom and put her up on a pedestal. My sister Jo Ann would tell you that the relationship I have with my wife Fern mirrors the one my father had with our mother. I'm proud of that. My dad was a true visionary who became successful at a challenging time in the U.S., particularly for African Americans—"Negroes" or "Coloreds," as we were called back then.

THE SOUND OF DETERMINATION

Have you ever heard something that immediately takes you back to a distant memory? Maybe it's a song that was popular in your high school years, a baby's cry, or a distant train whistle. In a flash, you're transported back in time to the moment when you heard that sound for the very first time. The feelings, the emotions, the memories all come rushing back any time that sound falls on your ears.

There's a sound I can still hear today, a sound that resonates in my mind any time I think about my father's hard work and strong determination. When I was young, my dad was diligent to have me by his side as much as possible. They say that some of our most valuable lessons aren't "taught" as much as they are "caught." That was certainly true of my father. I can't remember him sitting me down, saying, "Sit down, I'm going to teach you something, son." But I can't count the number of lessons he taught me by simply going about his business and letting me hang around by his side.

I remember riding with him in his old seafoam green and white Ford truck. As he shifted through the gears, he whistled. I can still hear his whistle in my mind today. One time, we were on our way to a dry cleaners/laundry that was going out of business. My dad was planning to buy a pressing machine at a fair price for his own dry-cleaning business that he'd started. The problem was that the pressing machine wouldn't fit in the back of the old truck. My father's solution was to drag the pressing machine back across town on a sheet of plywood tied to the back of the truck.

This experience made an indelible memory for me for several reasons. I believe I was only about ten years old or so when this incident occurred, but I can still remember the sound of plywood dragging on the asphalt as we drove from the southside of Houston to the northside and back. My dad was whistling the whole way. I could always tell when he was in deep thought. He whistled. There is no doubt he was imagining what the new pressing machine would mean to his cleaners, dreaming about being a successful business owner and providing for his family.

As I got older, I realized a few important lessons from this experience. First, my dad was undeterred by the fact that he was buying the pressing machine from a drycleaners that was going out of business. He wasn't even put off by the fact that the machine wouldn't fit in the back of his truck. He simply whistled a tune while he thought of the risks he faced. How bold was that?

Over the years, I've heard many successful entrepreneurs say that they found opportunities during challenging economic times, "making lemonade out of lemons," so to speak. My dad certainly modeled that attitude for me.

Secondly, access to capital was restricted for black entrepreneurs, especially in those days. We couldn't borrow money from a bank to start a business like others could. My dad didn't have the resources to buy a trailer to haul the equipment all the way across Houston, but that didn't stop him either. He was resourceful and figured out another way to move that equipment. Often, when I speak to young entrepreneurs about starting a business, I refer to this as the "sound of determination." I learned determination and resourcefulness from my dad.

It's a memory I think of often as I make hard decisions today. For me, hearing dad whistling, combined with hearing the plywood behind the truck dragging on the asphalt, became the sound of determination, hard work, and dreaming of success. And it's because of that memory that I learned to whistle while I work, no matter how hard the job. I imagine those sounds, and it's as if my dad is right there by my side, urging me onward.

MAKING HARD WORK LOOK EASY

My dad was the hardest worker I've ever known. But the most incredible thing about him was that he made hard work look easy. Dad was usually the person all the way in the back of his plant, doing the most demanding job in the cleaners, far harder than the jobs that any of his twenty-five employees, including us kids, were doing at the time.

I can still smell the steam as dad worked at his spotting board next to the boiler room, the cleaners' hottest part. When I reflect on that time, I can almost feel the heat coming from the boiler. It was so hot and sticky where my dad stood for many hours a day, removing the stains from his customers' clothes. Sweat rolled down his face, but I'm not sure he even felt it. He was so focused.

My dad exemplified servant leadership and the scripture in Colossians 3:23 that says, "Whatever you do, work at it with all your heart, as working for the Lord, not for human masters" (NIV). I remember my dad saying, "If you are going to do a good job, put everything into it." He worked hard to deliver the highest quality for his customers and, consequently, he was able to build a loyal clientele.

If you are going to do a good job, put everything into it. "Whatever you do, work at it with all your heart as working for the Lord, not for human masters." Colossians 3:23 (NIV)

Why did my dad work so hard, so diligently? Why do you think he was so committed to going the extra mile? It's because he was convinced that his primary job in this world was to provide for his family. First and foremost, he was determined to see that all our needs (and many of our wants!) were taken care of. For my dad, it was all about building a legacy.

My dad was a great man, and he's become even greater in my mind since his passing. But if my siblings and I were to ever have a complaint about our dad, it was the fact that he was always so busy. Consequently, we had no expectations that Daddy would show up at our school events. Over the years, he missed dozens of dance recitals, football games, and basketball games. We learned that if we wanted to see our dad, we had to go to the cleaners and stand next to him at the spotting board. We would talk, and he would listen and nod, doing the best he could.

But despite all this, on Sundays, right after church, we'd take a ride through River Oaks, a white neighborhood, to get ice cream as our fun time. Nothing elaborate, just a simple, little thing. But it was memorable.

There were no family trips out of town, except when we would visit my sister Jo Ann while she was attending Dillard University in New Orleans, Louisiana. On those occasions, our dad would leave the cleaners and take a short nap before making the six-hour drive in the middle of the night. I never really thought about this until later in life. At the time, there wasn't anything unusual about it. It's just the way things were. We drove at night because, in those days, Negroes would get stopped by the police if we got caught driving through certain towns, such as Vidor, a notorious KKK town in Texas. In fact, during this era, there were "Sundown Towns." I now have a better understanding of the risks my parents were taking and their strong love of family. No matter what, we were going to see my sister!

My dad was an encourager. For example, he encouraged us in whatever we had an interest in. He would say to my mom, "Elvira, go get it." When I was seven years old, I realized that I wanted to play drums, so Daddy told my mama, "Go get that boy some drums!" This "boy" is still playing the drums over fifty years later.

Over time, as with some neighborhoods, Sunnyside, the community where we lived, began changing from a wholesome, family neighborhood to one riddled with drugs and crime. It was through that stressful time that my father became ill and developed a heart condition. Mom could see that if they continued with the cleaning business, it would not be healthy for Dad.

So, it was my mom who eventually found a property advertised in the Houston newspaper. The place was not far away, in Somerville, Texas, and she showed the ad to my dad. After driving out to look at the property, they decided to buy it. A few years later, they sold Jones Cleaners and Laundry to Pilgrim Cleaners, a chain of dry cleaning and laundry stores in Houston. My dad retired, for the first time, at the young age of 52.

But my dad didn't resign himself to sitting on the front porch sipping sweet tea, watching the sunset. After retiring early, he and my mom stayed busy, starting their second and third businesses. Growing up in Louisiana, dad developed a passion for land and cattle. When he retired from the dry-cleaning business, mom and dad moved my brother and me to Somerville, where dad ran their 200-acre ranch.

A few years later, they purchased a small convenience store in Bryan, Texas. It was next to the store that my dad had a small three-bedroom mobile home. And it was into this mobile home that Fern and I moved after we got married and started having kids. I would say we were just getting by, but I'm not sure I can even say that. It's crazy to think about, but today, Fern and I live in a beautiful home just four and a half miles from that old convenience store and the spot where the mobile home was parked. Talk about a life going full circle!

PUT A PENCIL TO IT!

Besides being a hard and determined worker, my dad was also a programmer and planner, always careful to think things through before stepping out into anything new. I remember him often saying, "I'll put a pencil to it." He also repeatedly said, "Measure twice and saw once, son," then he would sketch out his ideas on paper. He was caught in the act many early mornings drawing on his yellow legal pad, listing his ideas for the day. Because my mom and dad worked so well together as a team, Mama almost always supported his ideas and found ways to help. My siblings and I remember that of all the attributes of their marriage, their teamwork was one of the strongest.

Plan carefully before stepping out into any venture. "Measure twice and saw once."

Because my father and his siblings grew up on a ranch, farming and entrepreneurship were instilled in him. He believed not only in working hard but also in working with the right spirit. His work ethic was well known to his family and to those he worked with. He often expressed his work ethic in terms of taking the initiative and not being complacent. For example, he often said, "If you find idle time on the job, pick up a broom and sweep. Do something. Don't just sit there!" My father carried this spirit into his dedication to being a successful businessman and role model for many. I remember many young black men visiting dad and asking lots of questions about how to start a business and how to be successful at it.

You could tell my dad was a programmer because he was always ready with a plan of action for anything in which his family was involved. I remember being newly married, living in Bryan-College Station in the mobile home next to the store. While our three kids (at the time) kept Fern busy, I was working hard, helping my dad in the store. It seems that somewhere in my dad's programming and planning mind, he expected that I would take over the store and ranch one day. Surely, he could see how much like him I was. My sister Jo Ann would tell you, "Eli looks like our mama, but he acts like our dad."

I did not realize just how much my dad and I were alike until we butted heads one afternoon while working together in the store. With each passing day, I was feeling the increasing pressure of taking care of my young family. I was keenly aware of my responsibility of providing for my wife and kids. Dad taught me that.

Finally, one day, I approached him and said, "Dad, I need to get a second job to support my family." We were expecting our fourth child and needed health insurance before Elicia was born. I approached my dad about the problem. "I need to get a second job to support my family," I told him.

"Why are you worried, son?" Dad replied in his typical planner way. "I'm taking care of your family. I'm providing for you."

His curt response was true. That truth hit home, and it hurt. Here I was, a grown man, college degreed, married with three kids and one on the way, and I still depended on my father to provide for my young family and me.

This was just the epiphany I needed to propel me forward. I had moved my wife and children back home to that mobile home because I was having a hard time finding a full-time job after graduating with an undergraduate degree.

What I viewed as a setback at the time was actually a setup for something bigger that God had in store for me. At that moment, I realized that my dad was indeed taking care of my family. I was helping my parents in the store but living in their mobile home. I responded, "Daddy, you'll never have to say that to me again!"

So, it was in the heat of that moment that I made a rash decision that my father probably would have never made. With no plan in place and our kids in tow, Fern and I packed up the few personal items we had, hopped into our 1976 Oldsmobile Cutlass Supreme, and sped off into the sunset. Well, not really the sunset; we actually sped off in a downpour and ended up at the Holiday Plaza Motel. I was at a personal low point, and my decision to leave the store hastily and without a plan had placed Fern and our children in jeopardy. It was an incident that showed me I still had a lot to learn when it came to programming and planning ahead!

ONE SPOT AT A TIME

As a self-made man who was a rancher, a community leader, a World War II veteran, and a small business owner, my father is my role model for being an entrepreneur in every way. In the Jones family, owning a business was a shared responsibility. So, when mom and dad had the dry-cleaning plant, you could often find me there, standing next to Dad at his spotting board, watching him diligently get stains out of customers' clothes.

That became a life lesson for me, so much so that I developed the saying "one spot at a time" later in life after reflecting on those days, observing my dad at the spotting board, focused on satisfying his customers by working diligently to get the stains out of their clothes. Like many entrepreneurs, my parents' Goliath was taking risks owning a business and supporting a family with no salary, living on income generated by their determination to take good care of their customers so that they would return and tell others about the great service they received at Jones Cleaners.

Remember to keep your eyes on the ball, on the most important thing. Focus on "one spot at a time."

I have given speeches on "One Spot at a Time," teaching working professionals about taking care of customers and creating memorable customer experiences. I have used the same "One Spot at a Time" talk to teach companies how to take care of their employees. When my dad passed, I had the privilege of eulogizing him at his funeral in the summer of 2008. My speech, then, was about how my dad lived his life one spot at a time. You will read more about this seminal concept later in the book.

These life lessons were caught from the time I was very young. They were rooted in watching how my mom and dad built their businesses.

THE LESSON OF AN ENTREPRENEURIAL MINDSET

When my mom and dad owned the ranch, I built fences and helped bale and stack hay alongside my dad. If you've ever lived or worked on a farm or ranch, you know that you must have a wide-ranging skillset to be successful. Much like an entrepreneur, a rancher must be pretty good at a lot of things. On any given day, you could find yourself fixing equipment, taking care of animals, building a shed, and then after a full day, spending your evening looking over your books, trying to figure out where to save some money. I didn't realize it at the time, but that experience of working on the ranch alongside my dad was some of the best entrepreneurial training I could have ever received.

When my parents owned the convenience store, I helped with the marketing. We had pool tables in a recreation room next to Jones Food Mart. I created a monthly pool tournament to bring the locals into the store to build store traffic. My parents showed me firsthand, and from an early age, that entrepreneurship meant working hard, being creative, doing tough jobs, and taking calculated risks. Because of seeing my parents model it, I have a high comfort level with risk and change. Fern and I have moved twenty-one times during our nearly forty years of marriage. That averages to moving about every two years. My wife and I bought and lived in several homes for less than a year during my corporate days because the companies would move us around so much.

With a firm foundation and legacy of entrepreneurship in my family, I became an entrepreneurial academic. I enjoy starting and building programs and outreach centers in the university setting. As a business dean, I supported the entrepreneurial mindset taught in our curriculum and celebrated my colleagues when they presented innovative ideas that would advance our college.

Use your God-given talents to help others be better versions of themselves. "...use whatever gift you have received to serve others, as faithful stewards of God's grace..." (1 Pet. 4:10 NIV).

In a special report by *The Chronicle of Higher Education*, the President of Babson College, Dr. Stephen Spinelli Jr., describes entrepreneurship as "inherently collaborative." He adds, "It is a way of thinking, reasoning, and acting that is opportunity-obsessed, holistic in nature, and leadership-balanced for the purpose of creating and capturing value."

Capturing value is how my father overcame the obstacles he faced as an African American in the 1950s and '60s when he chose to start his new cleaning and laundry business in Houston, Texas.

With little formal education and a lot of grit, he built a customer base by going door-to-door to neighbors in Houston's south side, collecting clothes to take to the dry cleaners where he worked. Ever the entrepreneur, my dad made a special revenue-sharing arrangement with Mr. Blanton, the owner of Blanton's Cleaners. After working his shift, my dad cleaned his neighbors' clothes and delivered them back to his neighbors. He shared a percentage of his earnings with Mr. Blanton for the use of his equipment.

Think about it. Have you ever had someone come to your home and pick up your dirty clothes, clean them, and deliver them back to your home? My dad differentiated himself by serving his customers this way, which resulted in building a strong following when he opened his own dry cleaners.

Eventually, my dad found a cleaning plant going out of business and bought the equipment to start his own business. Like I said before, with my dad, owning a business was a shared responsibility. Mom worked as a seamstress and later as the bookkeeper while Elaine and Jo Ann worked in the front part of the cleaners, packaging up the clothes for customers to pick up.

A CUT ABOVE

It is from my parents that I learned to serve others with the God-given gifts that I've been given. I grew up watching my mom and dad working together as a team and using their talents to help others be better versions of themselves. They exemplified 1 Peter 4:10 that says, "Each of you should use whatever gift you have received to serve others, as faithful stewards of God's grace in its various forms" (NIV).

My dad taught me that it is essential to be a cut above whenever you are criticized or judged. As an African American male, I've learned to live with being underestimated. This was especially eye-opening when I was a student.

For example, when I was accused of cheating on a test in the eighth grade, my dad came up to the school and sat at a desk next to me in the classroom while I took the next test. After I aced it, my dad proudly said to the teacher, "I told you my son doesn't cheat." Even though excelling and going the extra mile was hard, I learned from my father how to make my hard work look easy. It had become part of my training to show excellence through planning and preparation. The early learning experiences from my mom and dad helped to shape my values.

In the very same way that you have had the benefit of standing on the shoulders of those who have gone before, remember, there are those waiting to stand on your shoulders. Leave a legacy for others to propel them forward!

My father had a heart for people. He was a loyal and loving man, and he shared what he learned with others. He always made sure he brought people along and helped them through things. Several young men are in business today because my father took the time and made an effort to train them.

Mom and Dad made a lot of friends. Dad was an incredibly strong individual, and his commitment to life was powerful. He had integrity and an innate sense of the right way to do things. Sure, his path might have taken more time, but he believed in doing things the right way. He and my mom were my greatest mentors. And not just for me but also my siblings, his employees, and a whole host of others we may never even know about.

My parents didn't let circumstances stop them. They took risks, worked hard, and persevered as entrepreneurs and strong role models. Though they may have been afraid at times, they modeled what it looks like to run toward your Goliaths.

When my parents died seven years apart, each of them had two funeral services in two different cities because their friends and family, as well as hundreds of others who had been impacted by their lives, wanted to pay their respects.

FIVE SMOOTH STONES

1. If you are going to do a good job, put everything into it. "Whatever you do, work at it with all your heart, as working for the Lord, not for human masters" Colossians 3:23 (NIV).

2. Plan carefully before stepping out into any venture. "Measure twice and saw once."

3. Remember to keep your eyes on the ball, on the most important thing. Focus on "one spot at a time."

4. Use your God-given talents to help others be better versions of themselves. "…use whatever gift you have received to serve others, as faithful stewards of God's grace…" (1 Pet. 4:10 NIV).

5. In the very same way that you have had the benefit of standing on the shoulders of those who

have gone before, remember, there are those waiting to stand on your shoulders. Leave a legacy for others to propel them forward!

OUR FIVE SENSES: GOD'S DESIGN FOR LIFE-LONG LESSON LEARNING

After writing this chapter, I can easily see the myriad of life lessons I picked up from my dad and mom, as well as many others along the way. But many of those lessons would be long forgotten, distant memories, if not for a miraculous gift from God: our five senses.

Take a quick look back through this chapter and see if you can find some examples of the powerful role my senses played in my lessons learned. Here are just a few:

- **Sense of Hearing:** My mind can still recall the sound of that old sheet of plywood dragging on the pavement. To this day, I can still hear the sound of my dad's whistle in my mind. These sounds are tied to the life lessons of grit, hard work, and determination.

- **Sense of Sight:** Every time I see an old Ford pickup truck, I remember my dad's creativity and resourcefulness in figuring out another way to move a heavy piece of equipment across town.

- **Sense of Smell:** The smell of the steam coming off my dad's spotting board in the back of the cleaners is still filed away in my mind, easily recalled every time I remember the importance of focusing on the most important thing.

- **Sense of Taste:** To this day, I can still taste the creamy sweetness of that special dip of ice cream that my dad bought us kids on those trips to River Oaks when we were young. This is a reminder that experiences don't need to be big and expensive, but you should always try to make them memorable.

- **Sense of Touch:** As a boy, I learned that the big boiler at the back of the cleaners was too hot to touch. But despite all that heat radiating off that old boiler, my dad chose to work back there next to it. He was the boss; he owned the dry cleaners. He could have stayed up in the office and assigned that job to someone else, but he didn't. Whenever I think of how hot that boiler was, I remember the lesson of servant leadership that my father lived out in front of me.

I'm sure you have your own similar list of lessons that are still memorable today because you processed them through one or more of your five senses. Take a moment and see if you can identify the lessons you've learned and remembered because of their association with your senses.

Other associations are valuable—like these five women God brought into my life.

3

THE WOMEN IN MY LIFE: MY FIVE SMOOTH STONES

Thought-starter: Can you name the top "foundational" people in your life?

WHAT'S YOUR "WHY"?

What's your "why?" In other words, why do you do what you do? This is a fundamental question that drives people to think more deeply about their internal motivation. My pastor says, "The 'what' disappears when the 'why' is big enough." At times, what we're doing can be overwhelming. Remembering why we do it keeps us motivated to continue.

In this chapter, I share five of my loved ones and how they have influenced me and helped me uncover my "why." Each of these five women is a Proverbs 31 woman. They are "clothed with strength and dignity; they laugh at the days to come, speak with wisdom, and faithful instruction is on their tongues." They are my five smooth stones.

> *What's your "why"? Uncovering why you do what you do helps when what you do overwhelms you.*

FIVE SMOOTH STONES

In the story of David and Goliath that I told earlier, we learned that just before running toward the giant, David went to the stream and carefully chose five smooth stones for his sling and put them in his shepherd's bag.

In David's mind, what were those stones? Like the javelin to Goliath, those simple, smooth stones were valuable, essential parts of David's weaponry. Those stones were a vital piece of his strategy against his enemy. His sling wouldn't have been of much use against Goliath without the stones.

I am so grateful to God for the five smooth stones He chose for me to have throughout my lifetime. Time and time again, as I encountered obstacles, these women were there for me. Each in their own unique way, they have helped me defeat the Goliaths in my life. My first stone is my mom, Elvira. Next is my beautiful wife, Fern. My third stone is my big sister, Jo Ann. Fourth is my sister-in-law, Cindi. And the fifth stone in my shepherd's bag is my oldest sister, Elaine. Together, I think of them as my "board of influence."

> *Have you thought about forming a "board of influence" to help you uncover your "whys"?*

THE WOMEN IN MY LIFE: MY FIVE SMOOTH STONES

MY MOM, ELVIRA FOOTE JONES: MY FIRST SMOOTH STONE

My mother ... I'm smiling and tearing up now as I think about her. I'm so blessed to have this deeply emotional connection with my mom. I realize it's a meaningful connection that many don't have. My mother and I shared a special connection, woven together throughout the decades, right up until the time of her passing—a connection made from shared experiences and moments. When I think back to all the major crossroads of my life, to the points where vital decisions needed to be made, she was there, right beside me, cheering me on.

That's probably the very first word that comes to mind when I think of my mom: "cheerleader." She was always an incredible encourager. Mom was at every one of those critical decision points in my life—every one of them. I'm a momma's boy, and I don't mind saying it. I'm a momma's boy, and I'm proud of it! Even my wife knows this.

I'll give you an example of the special connection I had with mom. When she passed, I had the privilege and honor to eulogize her. I remember going to each of my siblings and asking them to tell me their favorite story about our mother. During the eulogy, I referenced the things they told me, and then I got to my story.

I remember a time when I was trying to find my way, still trying to figure things out. My freshman year at Texas A&M was so full and busy that I dropped out of college for a short while. I was going to school full-time on a prestigious academic scholarship, but, at the time, I felt like I was drowning. My oldest daughter had just been born. My parents needed my help in their store. I also worked crazy shifts as a DJ at a radio station in Bryan, Texas.

Finally, I told myself, "You know what, this is ridiculous. I can't keep this up. I'm going to quit school and be a radio DJ. I just have to accept that."

I remember, even in those dark times of confusion and helplessness, Mom was always right there at every moment to say, "Son, you're doing fine. Just keep going. I don't care if you want to be a clown. Be the best clown you can be."

Then early one morning, when I was driving from the radio station, where I'd been working all night, to the store to put in my shift there, I had an epiphany, a God-moment. I would not spend the rest of my life as a radio DJ. I would go back to school and continue to pursue my dream of being a first-generation college graduate, just like my big sister, Jo Ann.

I got to the store and eagerly told mom my news. "I'm going back to school. This time to finish. No more thoughts of dropping out. I'm going to see this thing through." My mom just smiled.

She said, "I knew you were going to do that. I can always count on you to do the right thing." That's my momma, always the cheerleader.

"OKAY, THEN. GO DO THAT."

Throughout my life, my mom was there at every one of those significant decision-making crossroads. I remember being in my last semester of the Ph.D. program and receiving offers to join three different universities, and, oddly, I got one from a company to return to the industry. Typically, doctoral students take jobs in academia. However, my career path took a few twists and turns. Before joining the Ph.D. program, I worked in sales and sales management for three large companies. I left the industry after finding my true calling. So, it was at this crossroads where my mom showed up again.

I talked to Mom about it. Should I return to the industry and earn more than twice what the universities were offering me? Or should I follow the traditional academic path of taking a job at a university to teach and write?

My mom asked me a simple but powerful question. "Son, why did you leave corporate to go back to graduate school?" Her question caught me off-guard, and I had to think about it for a moment. When the answer came to me, I realized that I'd always wanted to teach and write. I felt deep in my heart that I wanted to transform lives through higher education, and to do that, I needed to go back to school. I told that to my mom. She just nodded her head and said, "Okay, then. Go do that."

With those few words, my mom put me right back on course. She'd helped me connect with my all-important why. And once I realized my true why, I knew it wasn't about money or climbing the corporate ladder; it was about teaching and writing. So, my decision was made. Thank you, Momma!

My mother was always there at the crossroads for me, in the background, ever ready for me to ask her what she thought I should do. She was a very wise woman who mentored so many people throughout her lifetime. She made such an enormous impact on my family that she earned the nickname "Queen."

MY WIFE, FERN WALKER JONES: MY SECOND SMOOTH STONE

For nearly forty years, I've been blessed to be married to Fern Walker Jones. The Bible says a man who finds a wife finds a good thing (Prov. 18:22), and my life with Fern has shown that to be true, time and time again.

She's proven herself loyal and loving in more ways than I can count, and just like the "live in a ditch" story shows, she's unshakable and steadfast, too. To this day, I am so thankful that Fern stretched her faith while we were in that dingy little motel room that night and chose to show her faith to me at a low moment in my life.

Now I can tell you the story of how we met, but the truth is, I've always liked the way she tells it better. So, let's hear her version.

FERN'S STORY

Music brought Eli and me together nearly forty years ago, and it continues to bind us together today. We are still conquering the world in unconditional love. The start of our relationship shows how God can work through people and circumstances no matter how big the Goliaths are that are blocking the path.

At the age of twenty-two, the timing was just not right for Eli to enter my life. I was transitioning out of a devastating family crisis involving the death of my younger brother, Tracy, and trying to conquer my own personal giants as a young woman.

At the age of nineteen, I began building a career in Houston as a barber stylist and very quickly became a prosthetic hair designer, consultant, and trainer for one of the top hair replacement distributors in Houston. Although being a hair stylist was not at all what I dreamed of doing for a living, I was given a much-needed opportunity, and I took it.

My goal was to become an "independent success." Although not my "dream" career, my business quickly grew, and I enjoyed blessing many adults and children suffering from pattern baldness, alopecia, and especially those going through chemotherapy at MD Anderson. It was fulfilling and lucrative.

In 1977, MAJIC 102.1, an R&B urban contemporary radio station, went on the air and was very popular with friends and family. At the time, Eli was a full-time student studying journalism at Texas A&M University, and he was also working part-time as a DJ at MAJIC 102.1.

He had the opportunity to meet and interview many recording artists, such as Janet Jackson, Prince, Luther Vandross, Charlie Wilson, and Michael McDonald. He also served as master of ceremonies for music concerts in the Houston Astrodome and the Summit. Although Eli worked part-time at the radio station, he had quite a following with listeners. He was even viewed by some as a "celebrity-like" figure, although not by me. I couldn't have cared less, and there's a good reason why.

In 1971, my father, Bernard Melvin Walker, began his second career in broadcasting as General Manager of KYOK, an AM station in Houston, and he served as vice president of Shamrock and Starr Broadcasting, so I was familiar with the radio scene. Groupies ran rampant and male DJs were typically known as womanizers and druggies.

Groupies would follow radio celebrities around, usually in hopes of getting to know the music artists. It was a profession of drugs, sex, and rock and roll. My dad did not allow my sister and me to ever step foot in the radio station. The closest I got to the music scene was immersing myself in crates of 45s and albums that my dad would bring home.

I would play records non-stop and get lost in the music, singing my heart out. My favorite album was *Sweet Sweet Spirit* by Francine Morrison. I believe this established my love for music and singing.

Unfortunately, whether true or not, as a radio DJ, Eli fell into a stereotype that I was taught to see as unacceptable, so I had absolutely no desire to meet him. However, our cousin Dea Briggs was determined to match-make, even knowing how "Uncle Bernard" felt about the music scene and anyone in it! Although Eli and I had not yet met, Dea was very close to both of us growing up and knew how much we loved music. She always believed that Eli and I would be a good fit. She first convinced him of it, and they began their little scheme.

Dea had offered to help me set up one evening for an upcoming open house at the hair salon, which happened to be close to the radio station. That night, after we finished, she tricked me into going to the radio station while Eli was on the air, under the guise that he really needed to talk to her in person. I literally had no choice but to go with her, because she had also offered to drive her car that day. I was so irritated and extremely nervous about stepping foot into a radio station for the first time in my life! I threatened to stay in the car, but that was not a safe option.

I uncomfortably sat in the control room as Eli was finishing his last hour on the air. He played a certain rotation of songs set by the radio station's programming. Because I was very familiar with the songs, I eventually realized that Eli had broken rotation to play a different sequence of songs—love songs that told me a story. Most people don't know that Eli was the first radio DJ at MAJIC 102 to introduce the "Quiet Storm" to the Houston market and surrounding areas. Many babies were born in Houston that following year!

Once the shift ended, Eli began a conversation with me. True to my no-nonsense personality, I wasted no time in telling him how much I was not impressed by Eli Adams, his radio persona. Of course, the radio persona is part of the job to increase listeners and station ratings, but the persona was everything I despised in a man. However, once we got that out of the way and became engaged in meaningful conversation, I expressed to him that I could become interested in Eli Jones.

We spent the rest of our time at the station together in the studio, where the DJs recorded commercials. Eli played music, and we sang to each other, literally, "until the sun came up." A spiritual bond was formed that early morning in that recording studio. Eli won my heart that evening, and we became and still are inseparable.

> "I cannot argue with the Holy Spirit."

However, I was still troubled not only by the timing of our coming together but by the life circumstances we were individually managing. My parents had not met Eli yet, but my mother was aware of our "involvement," so I shared in detail with her my concerns to assure her that my eyes were wide open. Mommee looked for God in everything, and she is the reason I have such a deep personal relationship with Christ. She taught me how to see everything through a spiritual lens. I expressed to her that I felt the Holy Spirit telling me that I was to "help" this man with/through some things, but that I believed it was temporary. Her response was, "Baby, I cannot argue with the Holy Spirit." Well, nearly forty years later, we are still together.

Music is the universal language, our love language. Music sets a mood that affects the soul. Eli still uses music to communicate with me. Music brought us together and still binds us today. It created the rhythm for the drum beat of our life together.

That's my side of the story. Now Eli will tell you the rest.

Who would you place on that advisory board, and why?

EXPERIENCES THAT BUILD A LIFE TOGETHER

The life experiences, both good and bad, that Fern and I have shared have shaped my thinking, nourished my soul, and most importantly, have set the foundation upon which Fern and I built a life together. As you go through life with faith, I can assure you that the hard times will strengthen and grow your faith. Unfortunately, when I was younger, I had not lived life long enough to know this to be true, but I know now.

I'm grateful to God for placing Fern in my life to be one of my treasured smooth stones. Through the years that we have been married, we've experienced sharp twists, turns, and dark places in our circle and could have chosen to divorce several times. But we stayed steadfast. We've learned that when times are tough, it's a time to cling tightly to each other and run toward Goliath together! Fern and our adult children and grandchildren are my why! It's about legacy for us.

MY BIG SISTER, JO ANN JONES BURBRIDGE: MY THIRD SMOOTH STONE

Jo Ann and I are like twins. We may have been born twelve years apart, but we're so much alike. Growing up, it seemed like we were connected at the hip. While in the process of writing this book, I read drafts of it to Jo Ann. She's been so supportive and curious about what I was writing. She even teared up when I read her the chapter about our dad.

A DEFINING MOMENT

Jo Ann is the first one in our entire family to get a college degree. The fact that I even went to college in the first place is directly related to a defining moment that occurred when I attended Jo Ann's college graduation from Dillard University in New Orleans and watched her walk across the stage.

I was ten when my sister graduated college, and I vividly remember the graduation ceremony. I was too young to really understand exactly what getting a college degree meant, but I knew I was witnessing something special, something meaningful. I watched her cross the stage in her cap and gown, and I watched how my family celebrated her, the first one of us to graduate from college. I celebrated too. I was struck by the confidence she had, how she carried herself, and the look on her face as the dean handed her the diploma. She was so proud of her achievement. I could see her confidence all the way from where I sat.

It was an amazing experience, even though I didn't fully understand it at the time. But it impacted me to the degree that I remember saying to myself, "You know what? Whatever that is, that look of confidence that I see on my sister's face right now, that's what I want."

For years, the picture of Jo Ann walking across the stage in her cap and gown has been burned into my memory. The experience affected my senses. I saw the confidence on Jo Ann's face. I heard the laughter and applause from the audience. I felt an enormous amount of pride for my big sister. I felt this moment to the extent that it profoundly sunk into my spirit. I knew at that moment, "I've got to go do this!" That's the encouragement that Jo Ann gave me when she graduated from college.

That memory became a driving force for me, urging me to run toward whatever Goliaths might be standing in my way of earning a college education. I knew I had to go to college, get my degree, and walk across the stage.

Today, if you talk to Jo Ann, this incredible encourager, about being my inspiration to go to college, she'll say, "Eli, he bypassed me a long time ago. I only got my undergrad and master's degrees, but he did me one better. He earned his Ph.D.!" Her attitude reminds me of Proverbs 27:17: "As iron sharpens iron, So one man sharpens [and influences] another..." (AMP). Her example sharpened me and encouraged me to keep going, even when times got tough.

Besides helping you unveil your why, what else could the board help you do?

MY SISTER-IN-LAW, CINDI CLACK KAR: MY FOURTH SMOOTH STONE

My sister-in-law, Cindi, is an amazing prophet of God. I've often said that she's like those old E.F. Hutton ads: "When she speaks, everybody listens!" That's true about her. She's an incredible woman with a special connection to God.

First, she's a survivor. She suffers from so many infirmities that it's unbelievable that she's still alive. Her degenerative physical condition would confine most to a bed, but she continues to get up every day and push forward, diligently doing the next thing next. Cindi is one of the strongest people I know, not just in terms of her strong faith but also strong physically, especially considering all her illnesses. I'm not going to list all the things that she is physically dealing with here, but through it all, she has stayed strong by trusting God through her circumstances. Her faith is her fuel!

Cindi has also had to deal with the tragic loss of her husband, who died of cancer some years ago. His death left her with many challenges to overcome. She is such an example to me of endurance and fortitude. No matter what might be standing in her way, she's going to find the strength to run toward her Goliaths.

My family loves Cindi, and she is a vital part of our immediate family. In fact, the last several houses we've lived in have intentionally had two extra bedrooms, one for my mom (whom my kids call "MeMe") and one for Cindi. That's how much she means to us, and I'm grateful for the relationship we have. She tells me that I'm not her brother-in-law; I'm her brother. She also says that she's not a sister-in-law to me; she's my sister.

The word that comes to mind when I think of Cindi is "faith." Strong faith. If there's a David in the story, she's him. At first glance, she appears to be small and frail, too weak to go up against the giant, but she bravely runs toward him, nonetheless. She's slinging her stones, and she's full of faith. It's just incredible. Her attitude is: "I am not going to let you take me down. You're not going to do it physically, financially, mentally, or emotionally. You're not going to do it! You're not going to take me out!"

She's a tough survivor, and everybody knows that about Cindi. Full of God. When you see her, don't let her appearance fool you. She is tiny and can seem quiet and shy in a room full of people, but she's always listening, always watching. And when she stands to speak, you can see the power of God all over her. And when she speaks to you, you know you're listening to God. Over the years, this prophetic woman of God has revealed prophecies about my true calling. She has influenced me greatly and helped me understand why God loves me and chose me to do the things I do. That's Cindi, my fourth smooth stone.

MY OLDEST SISTER, ELAINE JONES PHILLIPS: MY FIFTH SMOOTH STONE

My sister Elaine is more than thirteen years older than I am, so we didn't really grow up together. By the time I started school, she was out of the house and on her own, but I'm thankful for Elaine's influence on my life. Let me tell you why.

Understanding my deep passion for music, my sister connected music to ministry for me. For the last thirty years or so, I have played and performed contemporary Christian gospel music. Fern and I have almost always had a band or some music group that we're involved with. We've enjoyed performing this kind of music together. For years, this music has blessed me, moved me, and inspired me in my journey with God.

Elaine is the one who introduced me to contemporary Christian gospel music, which has played such a meaningful role throughout my life ever since. I have Elaine to thank for opening this door and for encouraging me in this direction. This simple but powerful suggestion guided me to use this style of music to soothe my soul and inspire others. She's my fifth smooth stone.

How could they hold you accountable for improving your life?

THE STONES OF MY FOUNDATION

We've been talking throughout this whole section about the importance of a strong foundation. The Bible teaches us that only a fool chooses to build his house on sand (Matt. 7:24–27), and yet every day I have the occasion to meet people with no sense of who they are. They lack the strong foundation that comes from knowing who they are and where they've come from. They're aimless and adrift. They have no foundation in their life, no one to remind them who they are or to love and encourage them when they're down. No one to push them to be all they can be.

I was blessed to have key people in my life who served to be my strong foundation. As you will see throughout the rest of this book, there have been others as well, people that God dropped into my life at just the right time with just the right word. I'm grateful for the strong foundation with which God has blessed me. My life is what it is because of my foundation.

FIVE SMOOTH STONES

The book of Proverbs was written by King Solomon, the wisest man who has ever lived. The last chapter of this book, Chapter 31, has often served as a blueprint for a virtuous woman.

Specifically, Proverbs 31 describes at least ten characteristics of a virtuous woman, saying she will have a strong **faith**, a good **marriage**, be a devoted **mother**, conscientious about her **health**, committed to **service, stewardship, industry,** and **homemaking**. She will be a wise manager of her **time** and she will understand that true **beauty** comes from godliness.

> *Take a moment now and identify the "smooth stones" that God has placed in the foundation of your life.*

I've been blessed throughout my lifetime to have the qualities of the Proverbs 31 woman lived out in front of me through the women described in this chapter. Each of the five smooth stone women in my life is clothed with the virtues that King Solomon wrote about all those years ago.

Take a moment now and identify the "smooth stones" that God has placed in the foundation of your life.

1. What's your "why"? Uncovering why you do what you do helps when what you do overwhelms you.

2. Have you thought about forming a "board of influence" to help you uncover your whys?

3. Who would you place on that advisory board, and why?

4. Besides helping you unveil your why, what else could the board help you do?

5. How could they hold you accountable for improving your life?

In the next section, we will build on the foundation and discuss finding your rhythm in life. Being a drummer has taught me much about rhythm and timing, not only in music but in life. So, let's talk about the drumbeat of your life.

SECTION 2

FIND YOUR RHYTHM

4

THE DRUMBEAT OF LIFE

Thought-starter: Can you find exactly what you want to do in life?

FIND YOUR RHYTHM

I talked in the first section of the book about the importance of building on your foundation. Research on the topic of social support emphasizes the need to have family and friends to turn to in times of uncertainty or crisis. This helps you gain a broader focus and a positive self-image. It also aids in managing stress. Your network of people can also impact your net worth. As mentioned in the last section, my family formed the foundation upon which I was able to build my family and career. In this section, called "Find Your Rhythm," I will mention others who God put in my path to provide social support and key insights as I faced important career decisions.

At the beginning of your career, it's okay to explore different options. In fact, I encourage people to do so. A job could lead to a fulfilling life. This certainly happened for me. Do you remember the full circle image? When feeling your way through the dark times, it's important to remember to keep moving, taking steps of faith and trying different jobs, always moving forward, hungry for more. Explore your areas of interest. Early efforts can be full of starts and stops, re-dos, and start-overs, as you do your best to figure out what it is that God has in store for you.

If you're faithful to keep moving forward on your journey, you will eventually find your rhythm. When I use that phrase, what do you suppose that means? When I say "find your rhythm," I'm using it as a simile. I could just as easily have said "find your way" or "find your calling," but I'm a musician, so I like to use the word "rhythm." Simply put, until you find your rhythm, you'll always be out of step with your true identity, the person God created you to be. Let me give you an example of what I'm talking about.

A metronome is one of the most important tools in a musician's repertoire. It is a device that makes an audible click at regular intervals. The click's pace, or rhythm, can be sped up or slowed down by the musician. This audible click helps the musician or group of musicians play together and keep in time with each other. Without the steady beat, the musician can be tempted to slow down or speed up.

What's your rhythm, calling, or purpose?

I grew up playing the drums, so believe me, I'm very familiar with the concept of staying on time and on the beat. In most cases, my drums provided a steady beat, like a metronome, for my bandmates and helped us all stay in time with one another. With no beat, the rhythm becomes irregular and choppy, each musician playing his or her version of what sounds right to them at the time. This is a recipe for a discordant disaster. In musical terms, we call this a "cacophony."

I speak to a lot of undergraduates who are in the midst of trying to find their way. They're in the process of marching to the beat of various rhythms, trying to find the one that fits them best, like trying on shirts in a store. Many feel awkward and frustrated, realizing they are out of step, not making the progress they desire. I'm quick to encourage them, and this maturing process is entirely normal. You must learn how to crawl before you walk and walk before you're able to run. We all start out crawling. We all, at one point or another, need to find our rhythm. The important thing is not to give up, settling for a rhythm that isn't ours.

TIMING IS EVERYTHING

Have you ever seen kids on the playground jumping rope? One kid is swinging one end of the rope while someone else is swinging the other end. Like a rainbow, the rope arcs overhead at its high point before turning back down, slapping the ground at its low point.

Now there's a third child, the jumper, standing to the side and waiting to jump. What does she do while she waits to step into the swinging rope? Is she just standing there? Is she looking off in the distance, distracted by something else? If she wants to hit her mark and jump in at the right time, she must focus on the rhythm.

To make sure she jumps in on just the right beat, she watches the rope carefully. Some kids will even wave their hands, marking the timing of the rope as it slaps the ground. And then, when the time is right, when the rope is at the exact right place in its cycle, she makes her move. She's found her rhythm, stepping in perfectly, and she begins to jump while keeping up with the timing of her moves. Something in her mind says, "NOW!" and she steps in, even though the rope is swinging right in front of her face. She hits her mark, and it's a beautiful thing to watch. Who knew that God would provide such clear lessons on life from watching kids on the playground?

I'm in the process now of talking to my grandson about finding his rhythm. He's getting ready to be a freshman in college. He's at one of those critical crossroads of life, trying to find his way. Is he frustrated? Sure. Is he confused? Yes, at times. These are giants that stand in our way as we search for our rhythm. But I remind him, "Don't let yourself become discouraged or distracted. Run toward those giants! Keep your eyes on the target and mark your time. It will come." I tell him to keep on taking those steps of faith, always moving forward; you'll eventually find your rhythm.

THE DRUMBEAT OF LIFE

Life has a natural drumbeat. If you listen closely, you can hear it—boom, boom, boom—an uninterrupted beat, keeping perfect time. The trouble is, many people are not in tune with the drumbeat of their life; they're out of step and can't seem to find their rhythm. Or maybe they've found a rhythm, but it's not theirs at all; it belongs to someone else. They're marching to someone else's drumbeat, living someone else's life.

As you move through life, God has this perfect timing for you. Like the steady click of a metronome, God gives you an assignment at an important and an appointed time. That drumbeat of life marks the time for you to act in step with that beat. But what happens if you miss the beat, that moment to act? I've seen too many people miss their beat; they don't act at that appointed time, and they miss that defining moment that God ordained just for them, all because they weren't paying attention to the drumbeat of their life.

By finding your rhythm, you can get that sense from God that, "This is my moment. It's right here, right now, right on that drumbeat. I have to move NOW!" God has a specific assignment for you at a particular time. For you to know exactly when to act, you must keep on moving forward, taking obedient steps of faith. Like the girl jumping rope, you'll never recognize your moment until you find your rhythm.

Proverbs 16:9 says, "In their hearts humans plan their course, but the Lord establishes their steps" (NIV). You might be busy making all your elaborate plans and strategies, but it's God who will direct your steps. He will help you find the drumbeat of your life, the rhythm that is just right for you. When the moment is right, God will nudge you forward, telling you, "Here's your moment. Take it; this is it. Take action!" Remember, faith without works is dead, and when the moment comes, you must be obedient and act!

What if David had missed his moment in the Valley of Elah? When do you think his appointed time was? When do you think God whispered in David's ear, "NOW!" I think it was right at the moment when he tried on Saul's armor. The armor didn't fit. David wasn't going to be able to fight Goliath wearing someone else's armor. If there was a time to walk away from the battle, this would be the time to do it.

How do you know that you're operating in your calling and you're in step with what God wants you to do?

But David knew that he had to find a rhythm all his own. He was going to have to face Goliath his way. At that critical moment, he could have taken off the armor, admitting he was too ambitious, too bold, thinking he could defeat the giant. He could've listened to his big brothers and sulked back to his sheep.

But that's not what he did. He heard the drumbeat—boom, boom, boom. He heard the voice of the Lord, "NOW," and he ran toward his Goliath. David's life was never the same after that moment. David acted when his moment came, and here we are thousands of years later, still talking about what he did that day.

What about Esther, the Jewish girl made queen of Persia? When her moment came, she hesitated, until her uncle, Mordecai, challenged her with these words: "... who knows but that you have come to your royal position *for such a time as this?*" (Esth. 4:14 NIV, emphasis added) She put her hesitancy and doubt aside and boldly put her faith into action, and as a result, she saved her people from destruction.

I'm immensely blessed. I can think back through various times in my life when I came to a crossroads, times when I could have gone this way, or I could have gone that way, critical moments of truth like we all face. When I think about the decisions I've made all along my journey, sure, I've missed a few beats here and there. But overall, I've been blessed, stepping out at the right time, in the right direction. It is all due to God. He helped me find my rhythm and recognize my moment. He was always faithful to put a significant person right there at the crossroads, someone to nudge me in the right direction, encouraging me to act.

When I look back, I went from being a radio D.J. to the dean of a top-twenty public business school. I don't know how that happened! That was all God. It's not like I had a forty-year plan to be here now, living the life I'm living. I just did all I could to find my rhythm and step out in faith whenever I sensed that it was time to move.

> *It's not like I had a forty-year plan to be here now.*

I had a drumbeat moment while working at the radio station. With only one more semester left to earn my undergraduate degree, I received an attractive job offer from another radio station out of state. But the condition was I had to take the job immediately, meaning I would have to drop out of school. What a critical crossroads that was!

Poised to graduate from college, I got a job offer for a better position, a management position, at a sister radio station in a different state. At first, it sounded like a dream job. But I listened closely, and I knew in my heart that to quit school now wasn't my drumbeat. It was sure tempting, but I knew I couldn't take that opportunity. I had to stay the course and finish school. I had to walk across that stage and get my diploma, just like my big sister Jo Ann.

ANOTHER CROSSROADS

I'm also reminded about the time I decided to leave my well-paid, corporate job with Frito-Lay and return to school to get my Ph.D. Lloyd Ward, the president of Frito-Lay at the time, asked me, "What are you doing? You're on track to be president of this company one day!" Talk about a tough decision! But I knew my rhythm was to transform lives, and I knew that drumbeat would lead me back to school.

A very tough decision was made easier because I knew my identity. I knew I wanted to be in the business of transforming lives, so I left the executive position at Frito-Lay, along with its company car and a big paycheck, and I took a different path. Not that I heard every drumbeat, every time, but I'm sure I heard that one, and I give God all the glory.

I've been blessed throughout my life in some key areas, particularly regarding career decisions. I'm currently in my third career. The first was radio and newspaper. The second was sales, sales management, and marketing. The third is in academia, as a professor and a former dean of three flagship business schools. I've been in this current career for twenty-five years and have had to make some key decisions along the way. I acted on the drumbeats that I heard: "Here's your moment now, finish college," or, "Here's your moment, don't take that job promotion at a sister radio station in Detroit."

> *When you look back on your life, can you think of times when you missed a beat? You knew that you were supposed to do something but didn't?*

Finding your rhythm to me means you're just getting started; you're just learning to crawl. I'm thinking about the young people as they're just getting started. They're trying to find their way. They see an exciting opportunity and think, "Okay, I'm going to try that." That opportunity falls through, and they think, "Oops! That's not it!" So they try something else. The important thing is that they are always moving forward, taking the next step of faith. And with each step, they are learning more about their own drumbeat. They are finding their rhythm.

FIND YOUR RHYTHM FOR LEADERS

I mentioned earlier that drummers are typically the ones who keep the time in a band, just like that steady click of a metronome. The whole band moves together, along with the drummer, who's keeping the tempo, the timing. If I'm the leader of an organization, then I'm like the drummer for the band, taking on the responsibility of keeping a steady beat that everyone can follow. When I take on the responsibility to be a leader of an organization, I know it will be up to me to set the organization's tempo. You can talk to plenty of people who know me, and they'll tell you that a good deal of the time, I move at a faster speed than most. That's especially true in the academic world, where things move quite a bit slower than in the corporate world.

Over the years, in every organization I have led, I've been the one to set the tempo. I've set the example, demonstrating what our pace should be, our drumbeat. I tell my team, "Here's our rhythm. Here's how we're going to get things done." Leaders should be the ones setting the pace intentionally for others to follow along.

As I said, I'm a musician, and being a drummer and a percussionist determines how I put together my band. What does that mean? It means that before making my choice, I survey all the various talents of those around me. I look very carefully at all the different people and make a note of their specific skill sets. I'm very mindful that I'm not just hiring individuals; I'm building a team. I always want to develop with intentionality, making sure the team members' strengths complement one another.

In every new position I've had, I've changed up the players. It's a lot like putting together a new band, just as I did when Fern and I were working with our music ministry. For instance, I'm not just looking for the best bass player I can find. I'm looking for the best bass player *who fits with the rest of the band.*

Success depends on our ability to play our parts in such a way that we complement one another. As every musician will tell you, you got to have good chemistry in a band. If we have any hope at all of making beautiful music, we're going to have to find that tempo, find that rhythm or melody ... together.

In the same way, that's what I do when I'm putting together my business teams. I look at the personalities of the different players, the people I could put on my team. I always pay careful attention to how the individuals are going to mesh with each other. I'm looking for individuals who can flow with my style and match my rhythm.

How do you reconcile missing a beat?
What will you do differently next time?

As I'm writing this book, I'm currently on a sabbatical, an administrative leave. The only way that's possible is because I put a new team together months ago, knowing I would be going on this sabbatical. I knew they had to match my rhythm and be ready to take over the college while I stepped away for a time. I said to the new team, "We're going to find our rhythm when we work together. You'll find the tempo that I'm setting, and that way, you'll be ready to jump in at just the right time, and we won't miss a beat."

THE DRUMBEAT OF MY LIFE

When you're walking in step to the drumbeat of your life, there will be moments of truth; moments of action, defining moments when you're at a critical crossroad and an important decision needs to be made. When you find that rhythm that is uniquely yours, you'll find yourself in tune with God. You'll be able to read the timing and hear His heartbeat and know for sure that God is telling you to do something.

In fact, I believe that I'm in such a moment right here, right now, as I write this book. I told someone the other day that this book is a "bucket list" item for me. I've always wanted to write a book like this one. Sure, I've written books and academic research articles and papers before, but those were about sales and sales leadership for business. I've never written a book like this before. Writing this book is striking a beat at the very core of what God created me to do, and that's to be in the business of transforming lives. That is my rhythm. No matter what my job or current calling might be, I know it will always have to do with transforming lives.

For me, the process of writing this book has been a real moment of truth. Even though I always dreamed of writing a book like this, I had no idea how to make it all come together. I didn't have a plan, and I had trouble finding my rhythm for this project.

Then I started hearing people around me referring to the story of David and Goliath. It seemed like no matter where I was or what I was doing, that story would come up. Like a ship emerging out of the fog, the idea for this book began to take shape. I could hear drumbeats off in the distance. But it wasn't time yet.

The next thing to happen was that God began to bring people into my life, specifically people who could help me get this project underway, people who could counsel and advise, and people who could help make this dream a reality. I was listening carefully to the drumbeat for this project—boom, boom, boom. Now there was no mistaking it. I could hear the drumbeats loud and clear.

And then, at just the right moment, God said, "NOW!" There's no question in my mind that the timing was His. It even aligned with the already scheduled sabbatical leave, giving me time in my usually very busy and hectic schedule to focus on writing.

When the moment is right, God will nudge you forward, telling you, "Here's your moment. Take it; this is it. Take action!" Remember, faith without works is dead, and when the moment comes, you must be obedient and act!

Yes, there's not a doubt in my mind; this is a moment of truth for me. This is a drumbeat of life, and it's like God saying, "Here's your moment. Write the book!" So, that's what I'm doing. I'm taking that step of faith, and I'm operating at this moment, this moment of truth. I've stepped out on faith, and I'm writing this book. Action is required! Because like Esther, this book is "for such a time as this!"

Writing a book is the logical next step as I pursue my purpose or calling. What is your logical next step? Before you can figure that out, you must first discover exactly what is your calling. This process will look different for every person, but one thing is true for everyone: You must learn to crawl before you can walk and walk before you're ready to run.

FIVE SMOOTH STONES

1. What's your rhythm, calling, or purpose?

2. How do you know that you're operating in your calling and you're in step with what God wants you to do?

3. When you look back on your life, can you think of times when you missed a beat? You knew that you were supposed to do something but didn't?

4. How do you reconcile missing a beat? What will you do differently next time?

5. When the moment is right, God will nudge you forward, telling you, "Here's your moment. Take it; this is it. Take action!" Remember, faith without works is dead, and when the moment comes, you must be obedient and act!

5

DISCOVER YOUR CALLING

Thought-starter: At this stage in your life, are you crawling, walking, or running?

CRAWL, WALK, RUN

Each of us has a drumbeat, a rhythm of life unique to us. But one thing we all have in common is a transformational process I refer to as "Crawl, Walk, Run." Simply put, we must learn to crawl before we can walk. Then learn to walk before we can ever think about running.

The website Business Jargons refers to the five stages in the transformational process as *exploration, establishment, mid-career, and late-career*. They call the last stage *decline*, but I prefer the word *retirement* instead (www.businessjargons.com).

In their example, **crawling is similar to exploration**. Generally speaking, these are people in their early- to mid-twenties entering the professional work environment. They may have worked various part-time jobs up to this point, but at this stage, they are starting their professional careers. Typically, we have several expectations about the work that are idealistic and unrealistic at this time. People might be prone to make a few "rookie mistakes" in this stage because they're learning.

Walking is akin to establishment. This is the stage where we actually experience the realities of full-time work life and establishing a professional career. We begin to figure it out and hopefully begin to hit our stride. The age range according to this research is 25–35.

Running is similar to the mid- and late-career stages. This is when we begin balancing a career and personal life (i.e., spouse and children). In this stage, we are maturing and growing. It's almost as if the headwind we've been battling has come around 180 degrees and now has become a tailwind, pushing us from behind. The research suggests that the age ranges for these two stages are 35–45 for mid-career and 46–65 for late-career. Many people in this latter stage begin mentoring and guiding others through their mentees' life experiences.

Can you identify times in your life when you were crawling? Walking? Running?

Where are you in that progression? Are you crawling, just starting out, trying to find your way, your rhythm? Have you passed through the crawling stage and started on the next phase, learning to walk, developing your skills, mastering your craft? Or have you worked your way through the progression now and started to run, having become an expert, doing even the most difficult tasks easily, as if by instinct?

Recognizing where you are in this transformational process is vital. The road to success and fulfillment is littered with lives lost in the frustration of trying to walk or run without first taking the time to learn how to crawl. Everyone, without exception, must pass through these three stages of maturity.

That's why it's so important to stay flexible and open to change throughout this process. As you mature and transition from one stage to the next, it will require you to stretch out of your comfort zone. Let's face it, change is challenging, and stretching isn't always comfortable. It's not like a rubber band; you don't just snap back into the same shape you were in before the stretching. But that's the whole idea, isn't it? You're no longer the same. You're growing, transforming into a whole new person. When God stretches you, you never come back to your original shape. Like a pioneering trailblazer, you must learn to embrace the stretching, running toward the giant called Change and not shrinking back.

Where are you right now in this progression?

CRAWLING

I started my own crawling phase after earning my high school diploma in 1979 from A&M Consolidated. It was only natural for me to attend the local university in College Station. I was thankful when Texas A&M University offered me the Presidential Achievement Award, a full-ride scholarship, merely sixteen years after opening its doors to African American students.

On the Texas A&M campus, one of the many wonderful things about being an Aggie is the set of traditions and the core values of respect, excellence, leadership, loyalty, integrity, and selfless service. These core values are ingrained in us, and the expectation is that Aggies will live our lives exemplifying those values in everything we do. That said, it hasn't been an easy road for many students of color who have attended A&M through the years.

As with many non-HBCU (Historically Black Colleges and Universities) college campuses, Texas A&M has had its challenges in recruiting and retaining minority students. Some of those challenges continue to this day. For instance, if you were to pull the yearbooks from the time I was a student at Texas A&M, you would find my photo missing from their pages, along with the pictures of some of my fellow African American students. It is a hard thing for minority students not to be recognized for their scholarly achievements. When I was in the crawling stage, something like this would upset me. I felt shortchanged. As I grew in the Lord, I learned to let God handle it. He had more important things for me to do. This struggle would later fuel my work with the Ph.D. Project, a mentoring program for minority students pursuing their doctorates in business, which also assisted graduates navigating the career progression from assistant professor to associate professor with tenure to full professor. Our group is now helping minority professors who have been drawn to academic higher education administration.

ON THE AIR

While studying journalism at Texas A&M, I worked on the weekends in the small town of Bryan, Texas, in what would be my first of three careers: radio broadcasting. I longed to break into a major market radio station, so I spent a year sending recordings of my on-air show to Bill Travis, a major-market radio station program director, for his feedback. This perseverance helped me land a job at KMJQ-Majic 102 FM in Houston, where I covered all dayparts: mornings, mid-day, afternoons, evenings, and late-night shifts.

It was not an easy schedule. After pulling three shifts over the two-day weekends, I would leave the radio station at midnight on Sunday and commute 107 miles back to Bryan-College Station for classes starting bright and early Monday morning. Then, on Friday after my last class of the week, I'd pack up and head back to Houston to cover my weekend shifts at the radio station. I kept this schedule all during my senior year of college. It was grueling, but there were some bright spots. This was also the time when I met my future wife.

I enjoyed my weekends at the radio station, although it was hectic. After checking in on Friday afternoons, I'd pick up my assignments for the weekend. My work included doing my on-air show, recording commercials, and doing what we called "street hits," where we would broadcast live from our advertisers' retail stores to drive store traffic. Occasionally, I was asked to interview recording artists—some of the most famous people in the music world at the time.

What are some of the giants in your path as you stretch and transition from one stage to the next?

One of the craziest times I remember is when I was sent out to escort Charlie Wilson of the Gap Band. Now, Charlie Wilson was a famous guy in the R&B world, so the radio station arranged for a limo to pick us up. I was to take him to a club and introduce him before his performance. The plan was for me to interview him in the limo on the way to the club. The nightclub, I will never forget, was called Bone Shakers.

So, there I was, interviewing Charlie Wilson in the back of his limousine! I was surprised that he was so laid back and quiet, almost shy. I expected all this energy and hype. But sitting in the back seat with him, I could barely hear his responses to my questions.

We got to the nightclub and made our way inside. The place was packed, and the music was deafening. I remember thinking, *No wonder they call this place Bone Shakers!* We walked toward the stage through the crazy crowd, one huge bodyguard in front of me and another behind Charlie.

I finally got up on stage and grabbed the microphone to do the "Majic 102 FM" intro that I was supposed to do. Then, in my best FM DJ voice, I announced, "Ladies and gentlemen, Charlie Wilson of the Gap Band!" That's when I witnessed one of the most incredible transformations I've ever seen. As Charlie came on stage, I saw a man, who only moments before had been quiet and laid back, become alive with energy and presence. It was an amazing transformation to watch. Here I was, in the crawling phase of my career, getting to witness first-hand a guy who had been in his career long enough that he'd learned to run. He performed effortlessly and instinctively that night. It was an incredible concert, an experience I'll never forget.

At the beginning of my first career, I worked as hard as I knew how to so that I could learn as much as possible. I didn't want to crawl forever. I was ready to stretch for more, to be able to run toward my Goliath! The radio station must have recognized my hard work because in the summer of 1982, just a few months before I was due to finish my bachelor's degree, I was offered a job, a promotion to the program director position at a sister radio station in Detroit. I've learned there are always people, often in the background, who are carefully observing you and capable of greatly blessing you.

The job offer was a good one. Detroit was the place to be in the radio business at that time, but the station could not hold the position for me until I graduated. Online learning had not been invented yet, so I faced a difficult decision of choosing between dropping out of college to take a job promotion or staying on course with my goal of earning my college degree. I was torn. In the end, I knew what I had to do. I turned down the job offer to move to Detroit to become the program director for WDRQ, which was an urban contemporary radio station at the time. I stayed put, finishing my college degree as a first-generation college student.

Little did I know then or even immediately after this difficult decision that God would provide even more opportunities in the distant future for me to earn several degrees at Texas A&M University. I would later become one of the university leaders. I am so thankful to Him that I have enjoyed a successful career in both business and academia.

Today, at Texas A&M University, about twenty-five percent of nearly 70,000 students are "first-gen," which means they are the first generation of explorers in their family who are seeking to use their intellectual and interpersonal talents to accomplish academic, professional, and social growth in pursuit of a college degree.

What does "running toward those giants" look like for you? What is your strategy to defeat those giants?

THE NEXT STAGE: WALKING

Four months after graduation in December 1982, I married Fern, and, with the Detroit job no longer available, we moved from Houston back to my home in Bryan-College Station. That meant that Fern had to give up her career after four years of building a successful hairstyling business in Houston. I knew God had something more significant for me than working part-time at the Houston radio station and deejaying in nightclubs to make ends meet. I did not know God's next assignment for me, but I was ready for the next step.

After our "live in the ditch" moment in the Holiday Plaza motel, on a whim, I dropped off my resume at the local newspaper, *The Eagle*. The timing was just right to get the job, but my assignment was an unexpected letdown. I landed a job in classified ad sales, primarily business-to-consumer and "inside" sales, which at that time was an all-female job paying low wages at *The Eagle*.

Classified ad sales were commonly called "want ads" and were grouped by categories or classes like garage sales, services, and help needed. Unlike display ads that show images, want ads were the cheapest ads that the newspaper offered. Customers paid for these ads by the word or line. It didn't take long for me to learn that by asking the right questions, I could sell more lines, which meant higher commissions. Little did I know that classified ads would launch my second and most enduring career—Sales—and eventually lead to finding my rhythm and discovering my calling in life.

What's your "big picture?" When you have moved through this transformational process of "Crawl, Walk, Run," where will you be? What will you be doing?

Gradually, I found myself transforming from crawling to walking, and occasionally, even running. I began *to sell my way out of poverty* one ad at a time, and I am still in deep gratitude today for this wonderful profession of sales. As I intuitively began asking my customers questions, our conversations led to longer classified ads. My boss noticed my selling skills and promoted me to the display ad department. This was a business-to-business "outside" sales position. I was given a sales territory, driving to retail stores to understand my prospective clients' marketing strategies and persuade the store operators and owners to advertise in *The Eagle*.

This promotion launched my career in marketing. Remember, my degree had been in journalism, not marketing, so it was on-the-job training for me, with plenty of Goliaths in my path. In the face of receiving so many no's and outright rejections to my more traditional sales pitches, I remembered what worked with the classified ads and began experimenting with a change in strategy from the typical ad commission sales model.

Using my radio background and journalistic training in interviewing and asking questions, I decided to pivot my role as a newspaper ad salesperson into a marketing consultant position. I began asking strategic questions and genuinely listening to my customers' needs and wants. Many times, I even offered to help them buy *other* media, such as radio ads, that may better suit their business needs at the time, even if it cost me the immediate newspaper ad sale.

Through this trust-based approach, I built relationships and honed my sales and marketing skills. Because of this new strategy, whenever I recommended that they advertise in *The Eagle*, they trusted me and bought from me. I soon became a top salesperson in the display advertising department.

In my research and teaching years later, I would talk about these very early selling experiences. For example, when it comes to selling, it is vital to get to know the prospective buyers' personalities and adapt any communication to fit their personalities. By accommodating your prospect's personality and preferences, you will not only effectively capture their attention, but you will also connect with them on a deeper level, building long-term trust leading to improved sales performance. Through these connections, I made lifelong friends, built an expansive network, and grew in the sales profession. Gradually, I was picking up my pace. Now no longer walking, I was learning to run, eager to discover the next step in my journey.

FIVE SMOOTH STONES

1. Can you identify times in your life when you were crawling? Walking? Running?

2. Where are you right now in this progression?

3. What are some of the giants in your path as you stretch and transition from one stage to the next?

4. What does "running toward those giants" look like for you? What is your strategy to defeat those giants?

5. What's your "big picture?" When you have moved through this transformational process of "Crawl, Walk, Run," where will you be? What will you be doing?

6

THE DISCOVERY PROCESS

Thought-starter: Do you think that finding your rhythm is a decision that you make, or is it more of a process that you commit to?

The answer is that it's a little bit of both.

Finding your rhythm and discovering your calling is a process. Success is obtained through trial and error, learning as much about what doesn't fit as what does. Most of the time, progress is made not with a single bold decision but by a series of smaller ones that gradually point you in the right direction.

In the early 80s, I was doing well, achieving a certain amount of success and fulfillment in sales and building a good reputation throughout the area as a guy who could get things done. I was known as a good listener who could deliver results. But it still wasn't quite right. Something was still missing. I had found a good rhythm, but it wasn't quite *my* rhythm.

Fern will tell you that I am a strategist, rarely sitting still, always looking for the next move. Like my father taught me, there's no idle time; there's always something more you can do. I guess the fact that a couple of entrepreneurs raised me made an impact more than I realized. Because of their influence, just going to work at a regular 8–5 job didn't fit what I was used to. The hustle that I observed in my parents made me hungry for more to do.

EARNING THE MBA

After our youngest daughter was born, I felt that I needed to go back to school to get more business education. So, I talked to Fern about my joining the MBA program at Texas A&M. Very candidly, I didn't know where to start. Graduate school was a whole new world for me. There wasn't anyone in my family who could show me the way, so I took the initiative to go to the campus and talk to the staff. In the process, I met Dr. Dan Robertson, who was the MBA director and a real life-changer for me. He was another person God put at a critical crossroads for me at just the right time.

Dr. Dan took the time to explain to me the admissions process, including the need to take the Graduate Management Admission Test (GMAT). He counseled me on managing the full-time course load while being a parent and trying to earn a living for my family. I passed the GMAT and enrolled in the MBA program at A&M. I was once again a college student.

My father taught me that there is no idle time. You can always do more. What more could you do right now that would help you discover your calling?

THE HUSTLE

While still searching for my perfect rhythm, I realized how much I missed radio, so I began working part-time as a DJ at the adult contemporary radio station in Bryan, KKYS "Kiss" 105 FM.

Hustling is one thing, but now "bandwidth" was becoming an issue. Going back to school as a full-time graduate student and working at *The Eagle* and the radio station, all while trying to keep up as an engaged and involved husband and father, was proving too much. Something had to go. So, I resigned from my job at *The Eagle* and poured myself into the full-time MBA program while working at the radio station in town.

At the time, Fern and I had just one automobile, a little pickup truck, and we were living out in Somerville, Texas, about 20–25 miles away from Bryan. So, after a full day of classes at A&M, I would pick up Fern and the kids, and they would come to the station with me while I pulled a 6:00 p.m. to midnight shift. Fern would bring blankets, and they would sleep in the station while I was on the air. Sometimes it's hard to believe some of the things we did to make ends meet back in those days, but that's what the hustle is all about: doing whatever it takes.

While I was on the air, people would call into the station and request songs they wanted me to play. Most of the time, while on the call, I could hear a party going on in the background. While I was on one of those calls, listening to the party in the background, an idea occurred to me. In a flash of inspiration, I asked the caller, "Would you be interested in having your own personal DJ at your next party?" She said, "Absolutely!"

True to my heritage, I tapped into my entrepreneurial DNA and became an entrepreneur, deciding to start a side gig, a mobile DJ business, calling it Music Man Productions. I began to book gigs while I was on the radio, taking my little calendar into the studio with me and asking callers if they'd like to have me DJ their next party. This weekend business began to grow, and soon we were getting bookings for almost every Friday and Saturday evening and occasionally Sunday afternoon.

When I finally saved up one thousand dollars in discretionary funds, I invested half of our savings in purchasing concert speakers to enhance the new business. Fern blew a gasket! She told me I was "out of my mind" and wanted to strangle me! She was planning on using those hard-earned savings toward buying more essential things for our growing family.

Ultimately, Fern trusted that my entrepreneurial venture could work, and soon we were doing multiple gigs around town. The business grew so much that I had to buy more music equipment to handle the demand for simultaneous jobs. I even hired my radio station colleagues, paying them $50 to help deejay parties that we couldn't do personally because we were overbooked. My radio colleagues were catching the overflow.

That's a trait of mine that I've seen throughout my career. Not only have I been extremely blessed, but I've noticed that my overflow has been a blessing to those around me. There's an old saying, "A rising tide lifts all boats," meaning what helps me helps you too, and the better I do, the better you will do. I believe this is a principle of God's kingdom, the multiplication of success. I've found that this principle is a key indicator of God's presence in a venture. Cindi, my fourth smooth stone, has always said that she likes hanging around Fern and me because it puts her in a place to catch God's overflow.

Fortunately, by this time, my mom and dad had sold the store, and they were able to help watch our babies while Fern and I worked the business. Together we would load the gigantic speakers into our little truck, hauling equipment all over town to the various parties, then setting it up so it would be ready for the D.J. When the parties were over, we reversed the process, going around tearing down equipment, loading it up in the truck and hauling it back home, finally finishing around one or two in the morning. It was hard, heavy, physical work, and it unfortunately took its toll on Fern's back!

Those years were crazy, but at the same time, I could feel myself growing. I was expanding my capacity, gradually finding my rhythm, figuring out my calling, narrowing down what I wanted to do with my life.

FINDING MY ULTIMATE CALLING

When I returned to Texas A&M to join the full-time MBA program, classes were held in the new John R. Blocker Building, which had opened just a few years before, in 1981. At that time, it was home to the College of Business Administration. William H. Mobley was dean and would later become president of Texas A&M in 1988. By the time I had graduated with my MBA in 1986, Don Hellriegel, now professor emeritus of management, served as interim dean for one year, and A. Benton Cocanougher was appointed dean in 1987.

Little did I know that as I walked the hallways of the Blocker Building all those times as an MBA student, my photo would one day appear in the Wehner Building next to these tremendous leaders on the business school "wall of deans" as a fellow dean. It really is unbelievable, going from having my photo excluded from the college yearbook as an undergrad to, years later, having it hung prominently on the wall of deans. Only God could perform a miracle like that!

I can certainly identify with Joseph in the Bible (Genesis 37, 39–41), who went from being thrown in a pit as a boy by his brothers to being sold into slavery, then being falsely accused and thrown into prison, and finally serving in Pharoah's court, being elevated to second-in-command, overseeing the entire country. Some things can only happen when God steps in and takes over, and my life has been an example of that!

One of the most incredible benefits of our salvation is hearing God speak to us personally. The still small voice may come directly from God, or it may come through people that God places in our lives—in my case, people like Dr. Dan Robertson.

God puts certain people in our lives at critical moments, and He works through these people to open our eyes to our destiny. Dr. Dan was a servant leader with a helpful spirit. He came into mine and Fern's lives at the precise moment in time when we needed him most. He was also pivotal in my finding my ultimate calling in life: teaching.

Life is a series of unending choices, and to make the right sacrifices and decisions, we must be still at times to listen. We must seek, knock, and pray for God's discernment in our lives. If we miss these opportunities to listen to the voice of God, we may miss our calling. We must remain open to God's calling, even when it may not make sense at the time. Hearing from God is essential when trying to find your rhythm.

*Have you ever heard God's voice?
If so, what did He tell you?*

LAUNCHING A CORPORATE CAREER

Timing is important, but life often marches at a different pace than we may have in mind. For the next four years, from 1986 to 1990, the drumbeat of my life kept a furious beat as I launched a corporate career in sales with Quaker Oats. But it kicked off with a slow start for me, a self-motivated, newly-minted MBA graduate. During my MBA program, I met a man named Jose Garduno, a district manager in Dallas for Quaker Oats. I met Jose when he came to A&M as a guest speaker in one of my classes. It was this relationship that led to my first corporate sales position.

After graduating with my MBA in 1986, I worked for Quaker Oats in Houston for Dennis Maple, my district sales manager. Dennis is currently the chief executive officer of The Goddard School. While he and I shared a more formal boss-employee relationship, Fern and I became personal friends with Dennis and his wife, Donna. In fact, Fern and I were honored to have the opportunity to mentor him about marriage as he and Donna were just starting out. Today, Fern and I have known and shared a close friendship with Dennis for nearly thirty-five years.

STARTING OUT ON MY KNEES

At Quaker Oats, I was part of a sales team of nine people serving hundreds of grocery stores by doing merchandising and store resets. Following a new schematic plan, these resets are a large-scale rearrangement of the stores' placement of products. As a store shopper, you've probably noticed from time to time that your favorite products have been moved to a different aisle under another section.

Little do shoppers know that this moving around of products typically happens in the wee hours of the night, not by magic grocery elves but by manufacturer representatives, who help store managers reset the store aisles. Our main job as manufacturer representatives was to talk with store managers who would give us three to five minutes to provide a sales pitch on a new product or new placement of an existing one.

In my case, I would call on a store manager who was a moving target, running all over the store putting out fires. I had to work hard, battling against all those interruptions, to persuade the store manager to bring in new products from my company or feature our promoted products prominently.

It takes a level of warmth and creativity to convince a store manager to do this. I was careful to be well-prepared, and once I had their attention, I would size up the competition and use creativity to do a better job than my competitors. Understand the store managers hear from sales reps all day long, typically offering financial incentives, such as display allowances, to the stores for displays and stocking new products. I differentiated myself through service, taking the extra time to work in any new products onto the shelves while I was there in the store. Although store personnel typically do this job, I always offered to do it, showing the store manager that I was willing to go the extra mile, which I learned from my dad watching him at the spotting board getting stains out of his customers' clothes. Plus, I could ensure things were done the way I wanted them to be done by doing the work myself. The job could be both grueling and frustrating.

Very early one morning, I was on my knees moving bags of cornmeal and flour as part of a store reset. I was feeling down on myself and disappointed because, after all, I worked so hard to earn my MBA, and here I was, spending most of my time moving bags of cornmeal, flour, and fifty-pound bags of dog food around grocery store shelves. It didn't seem fair. And the more I thought about it, the more frustrated and disappointed I became.

Frustration and Disappointment reared up on that grocery store aisle that night like enormous Goliaths, daring me to quit. I mean, I was a college graduate with an MBA degree, on my knees in a grocery store in the wee hours of the morning, covered in cornmeal. At the same time, my fellow full-time MBA colleagues worked regular business hours in management training positions for banks and energy companies! Right then and there, I wanted to give up. Have you ever felt that way? Sure, you have! I know I can't be the only one who's had those kinds of feelings. The giants were taunting me, goading me to throw in the towel.

But God had a different plan! He sent me a couple of smooth stones to help me defeat those giants. One stone was a guy named Michael Crawford, who was with another vendor working that night in the same aisle as me. I was down on my knees, and even though I don't think I was actually throwing anything around, I was in the wrong place mentally, obviously in a foul mood.

Michael saw me and immediately felt what I was feeling. He came down the aisle and prayed for me at that moment. I'd never met the man before and never met him again, but I remember his name to this day. God used Michael Crawford and his prayer that very early morning to defeat those giants and pull me through. How fitting it was that I was literally on my knees already. But even though those giants were dead, another giant appeared. This one was bigger and meaner and more powerful than the first two. This one was called "Self-Pity." He said, "Brother, when you're feeling down like this, you need a ministry, which immediately took me back to Elaine's influence, connecting music to ministry. Months later, Fern and I started our first music ministry, Exalt.

So, God provided another stone for me to use against Self Pity's giant, my boss Dennis Maple. I called Dennis and solemnly said, "I quit. I did not get an MBA to do this kind of work. I don't mind working hard, but this job is way below my expectations." Thankfully, he said just the right prophetic words at just the right time for me to hear them. "Jones, don't be short-sighted. You are not going to be doing this for the rest of your career. Hang in there!" I immediately thought back on my days in sales at *The Eagle* newspaper when I received that first unexpected assignment. I was disappointed having to sell want ads, but I stuck it out, allowing God to stretch me, and I ended up becoming successful. So, I decided to follow Dennis' advice, and I hung in there.

Can you name 2–3 significant giants that you've had to face in your life? Did they get the best of you, or did you defeat them?

Sure enough, Dennis was right, and within several months, I was promoted to call on the regional headquarters of Safeway and, later, Randall's Supermarkets and Fleming, a wholesaler. Not long after that, I was promoted again to zone sales planning manager, and the family and I moved to Jacksonville, Florida. From there, it quickly became a whirlwind, as we moved our family several times for positions in Florida, North Carolina, South Carolina, and finally back to Texas, all in a span of two-and-a-half years (1988–1991)!

I went on to enjoy a career in sales and sales management for three very large companies. I worked my way up to positions that included key account manager, key account executive (responsible for two of the top-twenty-five accounts in the U.S.), zone sales planning manager (responsible for sales revenues in three states), sales manager, and zone sales leader designate.

It was in these positions that I discovered God's fivefold spiritual gifts in my life: I am a Teacher and an Apostle. The apostle Paul lists the fivefold spiritual gifts in Ephesians 4:11: "So Christ himself gave the apostles, the prophets, the evangelists, the pastors and teachers" (NIV).

As I conducted sales training sessions with my various teams, I discovered that what I enjoyed most about leading people was teaching. In a spiritual sense, some would say that teachers are known as "light givers" in the Kingdom of God.

Influence Magazine describes being a teacher as follows. "Teachers make the truth and knowledge about God accessible to all. They have the ability to break confusion and misinformation. They are strategic in helping people know the truth of God and how it applies to their own life."[1] I really like that definition.

> Do you know your spiritual gift?

I was no longer just crawling or walking, trying to find my way. I had found an essential element of my calling, and that was to teach. The wind was at my back, and *I was starting to run.*

Do you know your spiritual gift? As a leader, you have a spiritual gift from God. This is a gift that He gives to you, one that lines up with your divine creation, not a gift that you select for yourself. Leadership characteristics differ, so your God-given spiritual gift may be different from my gifts of teaching and being an Apostle. Each one of us is called to use our gift and to do so appropriately. Once again, the fivefold spiritual gifts are apostle, prophet, evangelist, pastor, and teacher. I encourage you to take one of the many online tests to discover what your gift is.

DON'T QUIT FIVE MINUTES BEFORE THE MIRACLE

We may miss our spiritual calling if we give up too soon or if the drumbeat of life is off beat. I learned this valuable lesson while on my knees in the grocery store. It was a lesson reinforced years later by one of our MBA alumni, Jeff Miller, president and CEO of Halliburton. I had invited Jeff to speak at my 2016 Dean's Executive Speaker Series at Mays Business School. That day he warned us:

Don't quit five minutes before the miracle!

It's true; if I had quit early that morning in the grocery store while down on my knees, I would have missed my calling in life. One of the biggest mistakes I've seen young professionals make is quitting just five minutes before their miracle.

As you imagine the next five or so years, what are some of the giants that you believe you're going to have to be prepared to fight?

As one of our Mays Business School students concluded, "The path to a successful career isn't necessarily a linear one. It will always be easier to seek short-term solutions when frustrated with the job but maintaining a long-term mindset when making career decisions is essential." Remember the "full circle" image we talked about earlier?

Perhaps, you have an internship coming up, or you are in the first years of your career and feeling like things should be moving faster. Hang in there. Don't quit minutes before your blessing!

STARTING TO RUN

I love to teach and utilized this gift while at Quaker Oats. Often, my bosses asked me to teach other salespeople how to sell the way I sold my key accounts. Through this opportunity, I found my true calling. I fell in love with teaching sales. I kept moving forward, putting my faith into action, taking new opportunities as they came.

Finding your rhythm is done through a series of smaller decisions that gradually point you in the right direction, not with a single decision.

From 1990–1993, I continued teaching salespeople as the sales manager for Nabisco Foods in South Carolina and, later, in Houston. Fern and I wanted to move back to Texas for the next chapter in our lives. I had begun to get the itch to return to school to get my Ph.D., but that didn't seem to make sense. Things were going so well for us; why make changes? But I was restless and looking for my next step.

So, once again, I turned to my good friend Dennis Maple for another critical conversation. I told him about my love of education and my interest in working toward my doctorate. He encouraged me to make the bold decision and return to school.

That's when I sought counsel from the two most important people in my life, my mom and my wife. After receiving their blessing, I decided to apply for the Ph.D. program at Texas A&M.

While in the process of applying to get into the Ph.D. program, Frito-Lay recruited me to be a zone sales leader, which entailed leading sales managers and running a distribution center.

In 1992, the drumbeat of life changed as Fern and I felt God's call to change the trajectory from being a corporate CEO one day to becoming a professor. It's always daunting to leave the security of a good job and a steady income and step out into the great unknown, sailing into the fog. The decision to resign from Frito-Lay and return to A&M came with a whole new tribe of giants that would need to be faced and defeated.

> *Remember, as you grow into your calling, the giants grow too.*

Throughout those years, Fern and I became well acquainted with the fierce giants called Fear, Insecurity, and Self Doubt. Remember, as you grow into your calling, the giants grow too. You'll have to face much bigger, much tougher giants when you start running than those you had to face when you were just walking.

In my case, I was happy to be running, but I had no clue giants were lying in wait, just up ahead. I was about to reach for something I, at one time, could have never dreamed of.

FIVE SMOOTH STONES

1. My father taught me that there is no idle time. You can always do more. What more could you do right now that would help you discover your calling?

2. Have you ever heard God's voice? If so, what did He tell you?

3. Can you name 2–3 significant giants that you've had to face in your life? Did they get the best of you, or did you defeat them?

4. As you imagine the next five or so years, what are some of the giants that you believe you're going to have to be prepared to fight?

5. Finding your rhythm is done through a series of smaller decisions that gradually point you in the right direction, not with a single decision.

---

[1] "God Gave Us Teachers: Why the Gift of Teaching is so Important Today." January 7, 2019

7

THE ROAD TO THE PH.D.

Thought-starter: To achieve success and fulfillment in life, it's vital you discover your true calling. But how do you know when you're on the right track?

The story of my Ph.D. journey began back during those busy, hectic days of my MBA program. I was carrying a full load. I was not only an MBA student but also a husband and father, a radio DJ, and running my own small business, the mobile DJ business, Music Man Productions. And as if that weren't enough, I was also serving as a teaching assistant for a man who ended up playing an important role in my academic career, Dr. Charles Futrell.

But just because he influenced my decisions doesn't mean our relationship was all smooth sailing. In fact, we got off to a rocky start when I found myself the only African American student in one of his classes. I still remember the day he pointed to me right before a big exam and said, "Hey you! Come up here and sit on the front row, right in front of me!"

I was embarrassed and humiliated. Talk about giants in my path! I felt like I was in eighth grade again, suspected of cheating. But this time, I didn't have my father there to fight for me. I made my way down to the front of the crowded classroom, sat down, and did my best to put the embarrassment behind me. I tried to focus on the task at hand, which was to do well on the test. I aced it!

Over the next few weeks, Dr. Futrell reached out to me, wanting to know me better. Eventually, he offered me a teaching assistant (T.A.) position. It was while working as his T.A. that he suggested I stay in school and pursue my Ph.D., which would take another four years on top of the two years it took to earn the MBA. Thinking back on that time, I was too busy to even consider another degree, especially a Ph.D., but Dr. Futrell was the first one to plant that seed in my spirit. However, all that was on my mind was finishing the MBA program and getting my corporate career started, so I filed away any thoughts of pursuing a Ph.D. After all, I had my wife and children to consider.

SUCCESS IN THE CORPORATE WORLD

I graduated with my MBA and was hired by Quaker Oats. Following the "on my knees" incident, I could feel God's favor on me, and I quickly rose through the ranks, which caught the attention of other companies in the industry. After a few years with Quaker Oats, I accepted a position with Nabisco and moved the family to Greenville, South Carolina.

Once there, Nabisco wasted no time heaping me with new responsibilities. They put me in charge of the lowest ranking sales team in the division based on the team's sales quota attainment: number 86 ... out of 86 teams! The pressure was on. The company expected me to turn this team around, and I was up for the challenge.

I put on my "researcher" hat and began to read everything I could get my hands on about motivating salespeople. It felt like I was researching and teaching full-time, just trying to retrain my team and improve their performance. I was so busy, and I loved every minute of it.

The team responded to the training, and improvement came quickly. Within the year, we rose from dead last to number two in the division. This type of success, so dramatic and happening so fast, was a real indication that the wind was at my back. I was on the right track for discovering my calling, for finding my rhythm.

Realizing my calling to teach and conduct research full time was satisfying, but it meant going back to school. I wondered if that's what Dr. Futrell saw in me years ago. He planted the seed to pursue a Ph.D., but now that seemed counter-intuitive. I was achieving so much business success; why rock the boat? In the meantime, while I was trying to sort all this out, I accepted a lateral move with Nabisco back to Houston from South Carolina, and months later, a job offer and promotion to join Frito-Lay, which came with a signing bonus. I was beginning to enjoy some measure of success, and I could feel the favor of the Lord in my life.

Your calling will come easily, even naturally for you, while others find the same tasks difficult.

"DO YOU THINK YOU CAN GIVE THIS UP?"

While at Frito-Lay, I had a familiar visitor come to my office in Houston, Dr. Charles Futrell. He had stopped by to talk to me about the Ph.D. program at A&M. We were able to talk a little, but the truth is, I was distracted, busy trying to run a sales force of a global company, with people coming in and out of my office and my phone ringing off the hook. Problems needed solving while fires raged and demanded my attention. I was in my element, directing my team. I was running indeed.

RUN TOWARD YOUR GOLIATHS

After a couple of hours watching me, Dr. Futrell asked me a question: "Do you think you can give this up and become a student again? Can you walk away from all this?" Of course, I knew he probably meant could I walk away from the salary and benefits, as well as the prestige and authority that came with my position in the industry? But his question made me consider something deeper and more profound. As great as this job was, was it really what I was called to do with my life? Although Dr. Futrell used different words, he was asking, in a sense, if I was sure that I had found my rhythm in the corporate world.

> *As great as this job was, was it really what I was called to do with my life?*

Rather than wearing you down, your calling will energize you.

While at Frito-Lay, the thoughts of returning to school continued to persist, so, as I had done before, I reached out to Dr. Dan Robertson, who was now the Director of Graduate Studies in the College of Business Administration at Texas A&M. I told him that I was thinking of leaving the corporate world and applying to the Ph.D. program in marketing. He encouraged me to apply. Unbeknownst to me, Dan reached out to the head of the marketing department, Dr. Paul Busch. He gave me his personal endorsement, telling Dr. Busch to "Give Eli a look."

That began a relationship with Paul that has lasted thirty years. Paul is another smooth stone. He has been my mentor and friend and one of the most influential people in my life. From the time we met, I've turned to him at every critical step of my academic career. When my dad died in 2008, Paul was at the funeral, consoling my mom and our family. He was also at my mom's funeral when she passed in 2015. Paul is the man throughout my academic life who has always been there. When I stop to consider the important milestones in my academic career, Paul was always right there for support, encouragement, and advice. When I think of my "inner circle" now, I think of Dennis Maple and Paul Busch.

I decided to go back to school. Fern and I would leave the corporate job and high-income and return to A&M once again. Throughout my life, Texas A&M has always served as my "home port," a nurturing place to sail back to, a place to learn and grow, where I could dream big dreams, find my rhythm, and prepare for my next voyage in life.

But my decision to return to A&M wasn't without some opposition. That's usually a good sign that you're on the right track. You'll get pushback from well-meaning people, people that you love and respect.

In my case, the pushback came from Lloyd Ward, who was the Frito-Lay central division president from 1992–1996. He tried to convince me that I was making a big mistake by leaving the company. He let me know that they were grooming me to become president of Frito-Lay one day. I told him, "I appreciate that you see me in that way, but I am being called in a different direction." Now that I knew my true calling, Lloyd's very generous words didn't take me off course. I was able to focus on my goal of returning to school.

I knew this decision would be a significant sacrifice for the entire family on many levels, some that we did not anticipate. But it also became one of the greatest miracles of my life, in which I finally found my rhythm.

Your calling will fulfill you, scratching an itch that you can reach no other way. Instead of dreading it, you look forward to the next time you get to do it.

Once the decision was made and the application submitted, Fern and I drove to College Station for me to interview with the faculty and Ph.D. students in the marketing department. On campus, I quickly realized that I was not the typical doctoral student. Unlike most in doctoral programs, I came from the corporate world with years of high-level industry experience already under my belt. I stood out from the pack and was looked upon with a great deal of interest. Several of the faculty expressed enthusiasm about conducting research in sales and sales management and teaching in this subject area. It is not often that Ph.D. students conduct research and teach in an area they did for a living.

Fern and I would be depending on my Ph.D. "student stipend" to support our family, and we realized that for this to work, Fern was going to need to get a job. So, Paul Busch hired Fern as a department administrative assistant, and she would help support our family during my quest to earn a Ph.D.

Dr. Futrell generously offered to become my dissertation chair. He would become my advocate, the one responsible for shepherding me through the doctoral program and signing off on my dissertation.

NEW LEVELS, NEW GIANTS

Never assume that just because you've broken through to a new level, you're done facing Goliaths. You'll find that the farther you travel down the path of finding your true purpose, the bigger and meaner the giants become.

In my case, I was confronted by two of the toughest giants I ever had to face in my life: Abandonment and Betrayal. It happened when I was about halfway through my doctoral program. It felt like I was picking up momentum, successfully moving forward. But dark storm clouds were gathering out on the horizon.

My relationship with Dr. Futrell had continued to erode over the first half of my four-year doctoral program. For the life of me, I couldn't seem to connect with him and had a challenging time trying to figure out how to improve the situation. For an out-going guy like me, who usually gets along with almost everyone, I was confused as to why I struggled so much in my relationship with this man.

Never assume that just because you've broken through to a new level, you're done facing Goliaths.

Amid this turmoil, the boom was lowered; just when I thought our relationship couldn't get any worse, Dr. Futrell said that he was dropping me as his doctoral student ... just like that. He told me that he would no longer serve as my dissertation chair with no warning and no reason given.

This wasn't just disappointing, it was devastating, and it threatened my graduation. A dissertation chair is a doctoral candidate's sponsor, advocate, a champion for the student's cause, and the one you could count on for support, direction, and guidance. Now with no sponsor to represent me, I would need to drop out of the doctoral program, halfway through it.

This was a problem I couldn't fix, an issue I couldn't resolve no matter how hard I tried. It tormented me with thoughts of confusion, hopelessness, and failure. The giants called Abandonment and Betrayal harassed me, taunting me with their words. Was I wrong to return to school for the Ph.D.? Was all the work I'd already completed just a gigantic waste of time? Would I even be able to find another sponsor willing to take me on now that I was midway through the program?

Like a lost child, I wandered the halls of the business college, looking for a new sponsor to represent me. I believe that it's no mistake that I eventually made it to the office of Dr. Paul Busch. I asked if he had a moment to talk, and he kindly invited me into his office. Over the next several minutes, the story of my impossible situation gushed out. Paul listened patiently as I unloaded all the hurt, despair, and confusion.

His first thought was to come in and serve as a mediator between Dr. Futrell and me. He thought the best course of action might be for him to sit down with us and work out our differences. That solution is typical of Paul's character and personality, always working hard to bring people together. But after some more discussion, even Paul could see that we were past the mediation stage.

Before leaving his office that day, Paul provided me with a glimmer of hope. He told me he would consider becoming my dissertation chair but would have to think on it for a few days, then let me know. I had lots of research and writing to do in the meantime, so I picked up my sling and ran toward the giants. I put the distraction and drama aside while I focused on the work I had to do. After a few weeks, which seemed like an eternity for me, he called and told me that he would do it. Dr. Busch would be my new dissertation chair.

This was one of those defining "God moments" in my life, another crossroads where God placed the right person at just the right time with exactly what I needed. Having Paul step into the breach and agree to be my dissertation chair was God's way of assuring me that He was with me, that He loved me and cared for me.

When you're done, you're amazed at what you've been able to accomplish.

STILL HUSTLING

Just because I was fully involved in the Ph.D. program didn't mean I had completely shut off the entrepreneurial part of my brain. No matter what I was doing, I was always looking for new opportunities to make some extra money to support my family.

At the time, Fern and I had a couple of Rottweilers, a male and a female. One morning, I walked out on the back porch with my cup of coffee and caught the two dogs "in the act," having a little early morning fun. Immediately my entrepreneurial brain kicked in, and I found myself wondering how much I could get for Rottweiler puppies. That seed of an idea grew into a nice little side gig for us, and we began selling Rottweiler puppies!

We found that about twice a year, the female would have a litter, with each litter averaging about eight pups. When the dogs were old enough, the whole family would load up the puppies, make a couple of signs, and head to a busy street corner in town. We would almost always sell out on a busy weekend, getting $350 for each registered pup. Let me tell you, that shot of extra income came in handy more than once!

What was funny, though, is that I would spend my weekdays steeped in academia, immersed in the Ph.D. program, researching, and writing on weighty topics, studying hard, learning to be a high-minded scholar. Then on the weekend, I was selling puppies on a busy street corner. One Saturday, a classmate happened by and saw me selling puppies. Sure enough, Monday morning, he was giving me a hard time, teasing me about my weekend side gig. I just looked at him and smiled.

I reached in my pocket and pulled out a huge wad of cash. I asked him, "How much money did *you* make over the weekend?" That shut him up! To go from being on a fast track to senior leadership roles in corporate to selling puppies on a street corner is, obviously, humbling. I had to get past my ego and think back on the times when I saw my parents doing things that seemed "beneath" them to accomplish bigger goals, bigger dreams.

I remember when I was in the backyard looking over the newest litter of pups and making sure the momma was doing alright. My dad was just leaning on the fence watching me, sucking his teeth, which is always what he did when he was deep in thought.

He finally asked me, "Now, remind me again, how many litters does she have a year?" I told him two. "And how many puppies in each litter?" I told him about eight. "And how much do you get for a puppy?" I told him $350. He sucked his teeth some more and then shook his head and said, "Here I am, in my 70s, working my tail off caring for a 200-acre farm, trying to raise a herd of cattle, and I'm only getting $350 for a calf! I'm in the wrong business!"

Eventually, he and my mom sold off all their cattle and followed my lead. They built a kennel and started selling Rottweilers and Dobermans. My mom had someone help her set up a website, and with that new platform in place, she began selling puppies to a much larger audience than what she could find on a busy street corner. Before long, she was selling to people all over the place. Mom even began inquiring about ordering semen from dog breeders as far away as Germany. It was ironic—I had spent my whole life following their example, and this was one case in which they followed mine.

ANOTHER CROSSROADS

At the end of the doctoral program, I received several job offers to return to the corporate world. Getting them, particularly a very tempting one from Coors, presented me with another crossroads moment. Would I remain faithful to my calling to teach and transform lives in academia, or would I go for the high salary, company car, and other perks that came with the corporate job?

Because I knew my calling, the decision had already been made. I would become an "entrepreneurial academic" and pursue a career in academia through which I could fulfill my calling of transforming lives through teaching. Once again, my precious momma was there at the crossroads to encourage me and affirm my decision. She told me, "I knew you'd make the right decision. You went to school with a purpose, and that was to become an academic. Now it's time to follow through and finish strong."

I knew I had found my rhythm, the true calling of my life.

When it's your calling, you realize that it's not you in the first place. It's God within you!

MORE INFLUENTIAL ACADEMIC ROLE MODELS

STEPHEN MCDANIEL: A DEVOUT CHRISTIAN PROFESSOR WITNESSING AT A SECULAR UNIVERSITY

Dr. Mac, as he became known, got this nickname from Fern. He is such a wonderful man and someone else we adore. Initially, he pushed back a little when Fern started calling Dr. McDaniel "Dr. Mac," but Fern persisted, even though she knew it made him a little uncomfortable. Eventually, he came to accept the nickname in the spirit in which it was given, a term of endearment. Dr. Mac is a man who doesn't need all the formalities. He's a man of God, and his love of Christ and his love for his family is all that truly matters to him.

I observed Dr. Mac teaching students. Without exception, everyone around him knows him as a man of God. It's not necessarily what he says; it's how he behaves and the way he carries himself that demonstrates his walk of faith. In fact, he's not outspoken at all. He's gentle and caring. He made an indelible impact on Fern and me. Eighteen years after I graduated, we returned to A&M, and he was one of the first to welcome us home.

LEN BERRY: A TEACHING ROLE MODEL

To be one of the best in baseball, they say you must master "the five tools," which are speed, hitting for power, hitting for average, fielding, and arm strength. Many good ballplayers may master two or three of these tools, but the very best will excel at all five.

Academia has its version of this truism. To be one of the best professors and an effective administrator, you must learn to master four key skills: research, teaching, service, and administration. You can be a good teacher or a good researcher and be considered successful, but the best will strive to master all four.

I learned this profound truth from Dr. Len Berry, who is the most cited professor at Texas A&M based on research publications. Not only did he teach this principle, but he also modeled it. Dr. Berry set the example that you could be good in all those areas, and it was an example that completely changed the way I approached my career. Ever since meeting Len, I've been inspired to sharpen my skills in each of the four areas. I may be a dean emeritus, an endowed chair, and a tenured professor, but I still wake up every day with the desire to be better, all because of the example set by Dr. Len Berry.

FIVE SMOOTH STONES

Over the last few chapters, we've talked all about the importance of finding your rhythm. We've looked at examples from scripture and from my own life of how important it is to discover your true calling in life. But how do you know when you've found your calling? How can you be sure if you're even on the right track?

I believe there are at least five ways to determine whether you've found your rhythm, your true calling. These five ways are our "smooth stones" as we close out this section.

1. The first way is that your calling will come easily, even naturally for you, while others find the same tasks difficult.

2. Next, rather than wearing you down, your calling will energize you.

3. Your calling will fulfill you, scratching an itch that you can reach no other way. Instead of dreading it, you look forward to the next time you get to do it.

4. When you're done, you're amazed at what you've been able to accomplish.

5. When it's your calling, you realize that it's not you in the first place. It's God within you!

Where are you in this progression?
I was about to discover just how big God is.

SECTION 3
DARE TO BELIEVE

8

ANCHOR AND FLOAT

Thought-starter: What happens between the moment you find your calling and the moment you step into it?

Most Bible scholars agree that David was still relatively young when the prophet Samuel singled him out from his brothers and anointed him king of Israel. It's almost certain that David was under the age of fifteen, maybe as young as ten years old (1 Sam. 16).

What do you think? Did David's life change much after Samuel packed up his anointing oil and left the house? Did David immediately stick some clothes in a travel bag, saddle the donkey, and make his way to the palace, ready to replace King Saul on the throne?

I'm pretty sure the shepherd boy's head was spinning too much to get any sleep that night. Maybe he imagined the sounds of an adoring crowd shouting his name. I'm also pretty sure that when David got up in the morning, nothing had changed. He still had chores to do. He got up and made his way to the distant hills to watch over his father's sheep. The only shouting crowd was a flock of sheep bleating for greener pastures.

Just a few years later, while still a teenager, David defeated Goliath with a sling and stone, and a legend was born (1 Sam. 17). But is David now exalted as the new king? I'm sure David thought that God would make him king, especially now, on the heels of a tremendous victory. But it was not to be, not yet. David does make his way to the royal palace but not as the king. He's made a servant, a musician, to play his harp for the king.

Years go by. Challenging, difficult years. Years in which David was never lauded as the new king. Quite the opposite. Instead, he was tormented and chased all over the kingdom by a jealous King Saul, who was trying to kill him! How many nights did David fall asleep with one prayer on his lips, "How long, oh Lord?"

---

*Is there a pivotal decision you need to make—
a dream you need to let go of?*

Have you ever cried that same prayer heavenward? "How long, oh Lord? I know you've called me for a purpose, but when Lord, when will I begin to see the things that you've promised?" Sound familiar? How many times have you thought you've found your rhythm and thought you were ready to step into your calling, only to have momentum halted in its tracks? Like a plane prepared for takeoff, just sitting on the runway idling with no clearance yet to gun the engines, you're forced to linger, wondering when the dream is supposed to come true.

In David's case, years had to pass, a long decade or more. 2 Samuel 5:4 leaves no doubt as to how old he was when he finally assumed the throne: "David was thirty years old when he became king, and he reigned forty years" (NIV).

David had been diligent in building his foundation during the years of watching over his father's sheep. He'd been anointed king, thought he'd found his rhythm, first in defeating Goliath, then in leading his "mighty men" into battle. But he still had to endure the furnace of waiting, the hardship of not knowing, before he was ready to become the king of Israel.

Through it all, David dared to believe that God was faithful. He dared to believe that what God promised all those years before, He would bring to pass. David knew God would do the things He promised He would do.

THE GOLIATH CALLED WAITING

Waiting is one of the toughest giants we have to face on our journey of faith. If you've walked with God for any time at all, you've been confronted by this menacing giant. He is far fiercer than others we may face because he never comes alone. He chooses to attack with his brothers Fear, Impatience, and Doubt. To defeat this giant, you must be patient and steadfast. Like David, you have to dare to believe that no matter how long it may take, God is working on your behalf, and He will fulfill His promises.

No one in my life demonstrates this tenacity—this patient and persistent faith in God—like my wife, Fern. Margaret Thatcher may have been known as the "Iron Lady," but I'm sure that Fern could've given her a run for her money! Fern is steadfast like no one I've ever known, holding on, daring to believe, no matter how long it takes.

Remember, Fern wasn't just sitting around biding her time, waiting to get married when I walked into her life. She was establishing herself as a successful independent businesswoman, designing wigs for cancer patients at the MD Anderson Cancer Center in Houston. Fern had grown her business from being a hairstylist to being a prosthetic hair designer. Fern was a consultant and trainer for one of Houston's top hair replacement distributors. In true entrepreneurial fashion, she was on the cusp of launching her own career.

But she put all that on hold, choosing instead to marry me and raise our kids. She sacrificed her dreams, daring to believe that God had something far more significant in store for her.

I know this story by heart, but it's not my story to tell. I want Fern to share her powerful testimony with you.

How has the giant called Waiting come against you in the past? Do you feel successful in the battle against him?

FERN TELLS HER STORY

1987 was such a difficult year for me, and I sometimes refer to it as my "boxing with God" moment. That's the year I finally decided to let go of my dreams and trust that God would be faithful to fulfill His promises. One pivotal day in 1987, after putting up a fight, I knew in my heart that God was asking me to let go, and I finally said, "Yes," because that's what I do. I say "yes" to God.

But I was not naïve. I knew that I would have to make some bold decisions that were going to require sacrifices and complete trust in God. I was keenly aware that saying "yes" to God meant saying "no" to many other things. Letting go was a painful sacrifice for me.

But through all the pain, I learned not to focus on the sacrifice but rather on the obedient steps I was taking. I became keenly acquainted with a verse from scripture I'd known since I was a young girl: "To obey is better than sacrifice" (1 Sam. 15:22 NIV). When the focus is on the act of obedience instead of what you gave up, it no longer feels like a sacrifice.

That experience taught me that yielding to God's voice is not a formula for instant gratification. But because of my obedience to let go of what I wanted, I felt deep in my spirit that God had a much greater plan for me. I didn't know precisely what those promises were yet, but I knew that I would recognize them when I saw them. People may plan their way, but the Lord directs their steps (Prov. 16:9).

When I finally let go and yielded to His voice to put my career dreams on hold, I had to totally lean on God because I was quite vulnerable. My mother died in 1985, so I had to trust and depend on God to teach me and guide me through His new plan for me.

Candidly, there were seasons of regret, but God was faithful to remind me of His promises. As I matured in my walk with God, He flooded my soul with contentment, which gave me a sense of fulfillment in what I was doing for Him by serving Eli and our children.

The only place we can really find true fulfillment and contentment is in Christ. True contentment isn't something that we can ever find in things, people, or even our careers, which can often be confused with our own identity. God promises us in 1 Timothy 6:6 that "godliness with contentment is great gain" (NIV). When we give up striving to find our identity in anything but Christ and Him alone, He is always faithful to rush in with His gift of divine contentment.

I made the decision to let go of my dreams almost forty years ago, daring to believe that God would come through on my behalf. That's when I heard His still and quiet voice telling me He would fulfill my dreams, and I would have everything that was predestined for me. Today I am blessed with a life I could have never imagined that night all those years ago in the radio studio when Eli and I stayed up talking and sharing music together.

Boxing with God in 1987 was a pivotal moment for me. I had said "yes" to God. I also had to exercise a great deal of patience over the years. Little did I know that the fulfillment of his promises wouldn't begin until decades later when I had the chance to meet a man named Alvertis Isbell.

Alvertis Isbell, who is known by his industry name as Al Bell, is a renowned music executive, producer, and songwriter, and became the owner of Stax Records. Al Bell is best known for his promotional efforts that drove the "Memphis sound" internationally and made Stax the second-largest African American–owned business in the 1970s. Al Bell helped shape the careers of such artists as the Staple Singers and Isaac Hayes. Later, he joined Berry Gordy at Motown.

What people may not be aware of is that Alvertis Isbell is a man that from the age of nineteen purposed in his heart to study and walk in the principles, precepts, and purpose of Christ. One of my favorite quotes from him is: "I listen, I learn, I grow (organically), and I support." Al Bell is a genius and a giant in the music industry, and as a low-profile servant leader, he has and continues to support the advancement of humanity. Al has become a close friend to Eli and me through the years.

Meeting Al Bell was a life-changing God-orchestrated moment for me. My inspiration to begin writing songs came from him. Once, after he heard me sing, and we'd become acquainted, he said, "Fern, not only are you a singer, but you are also a writer and a producer ... you just don't know it yet!" He described me as a unique and rare "spirit." I guess it takes one to know one!

Though I'd grown up loving music and singing, I'd never written a song and certainly never recorded anything professionally. I do not play an instrument, nor do I read music, but his words touched something deep inside me that day. When God sends someone across your path to tell you something, intending to awaken something dormant in your soul, you may not even be aware of it at the time, but your spirit immediately receives it. That thing is then activated within you. That day, I dared to believe what Al told me was from God, which planted seeds of destiny in my soul. After many years of waiting, I finally sensed that God was fulfilling His promises.

*What is it that God is calling
you to dare to believe?*

For the first time in my life, I began to see myself as a writer, looking for inspiration everywhere I went. Eli and I were living in Northwest Arkansas and took the family on a short trip to Bentonville to visit the Walton Museum. While there, I read the famous quote attributed to Helen Walton, the wife of Sam Walton, the Wal-Mart founder. She said, "It's not what you gather but what you scatter that tells what kind of life you have lived." I was moved by her words and immediately inspired to write a song, calling it "Scatter."

> It's not what you gather, it's what you scatter that
>   tells what kind of life you've lived
> It's not what you gather, it's what you scatter that
>   bears fruit from what you give
>
> The life you live will define your legacy
> Not by what you HAVE, but by what you LEAVE
>
> From EVERY seed you plant, you WILL reap what
>   you sow
> So, give from your heart, great blessings follow
>
> It's not what you gather, it's what you scatter that
>   tells what kind of life you've lived
> It's not what you gather, it's what you scatter that
>   bears fruit from what you give

Within each of us are unique gifts to share
Our willingness to serve may someday impact the world

When the needs of one or many become what really matters
GREATNESS can begin from just one of the seeds we scattered

It's not what you gather, it's what you scatter that tells what kind of life you've lived
It's not what you gather, it's what you scatter that bears fruit from what you give

Search your heart for your Purpose in life...the thing that comes easy to you
It is there you will find that the greatest gift is the gift of giving YOU!

It's not what you gather, it's what you scatter that tells what kind of life you've lived
It's not what you gather, it's what you scatter that bears fruit from what you give.

I couldn't wait to share the lyrics to my new song with Al. But after "studying the lyrics," as he would say, his response was, "This is good, Fern, but this isn't *it*. This effort isn't coming from inside of you." I was disappointed but not discouraged. I continued to look for what God may want me to write about.

> *I was disappointed but not discouraged.*

One day, shortly after this, I was talking to Al about my journey, particularly the difficult decisions I made back in 1987. He listened intensely and then responded, "*That!* Write that! That's coming from deep inside of you. I want to hear Fern ... just tell your story ... it will bless people." Al took the time to mentor me professionally and spiritually. After one candid conversation loaded with valuable information and spiritual wisdom, I wrote the lyrics to "Dare to Believe." It is the first song that I wrote, professionally produced, published, and have performed.

"Dare to Believe"

I had to reach way deep within
To find that place where all my dreams began,
I thought those dreams were lost because
I left them with the child I once was
I had to put my dreams on hold then
As a totally new plan unfolded
But I heard a still and quiet voice say
That my dreams would be fulfilled one day
I dare to believe
And I know I'll receive EVERYTHING predestined
    for me
Where my faith takes me
I dare to believe!
Oh, I dare to believe
And I know I'll achieve EVERYTHING that I choose
    to be
My gifts make room for me
So, I dare to believe
So, just yield to the power of the voice inside, and
    you will be amazed to find
That every step we take in life, you see, is a path to
    our destiny
It doesn't matter if you're young or old or if your
    life has yet to unfold
I can tell you that it's never too late; dreams don't
    have an expiration date

We did not create our heart's desires; they were divinely placed in us
This is why we can't let go
This is why we must ...
DARE TO BELIEVE

How does waiting on God make you feel?

ANCHOR AND FLOAT STRATEGY

In 1986, after Eli finished his MBA at Texas A&M, we moved back to Houston so he could start his new career in the consumer-packaged goods industry with Quaker Oats. We had been away from Houston for three years, and things had significantly changed since we left. The Houston economy was still reeling from an oil bust that affected everyone, from CEOs to men and women in hard hats and work boots at the refineries.

Eli was just starting his corporate career, and I was looking forward to stepping back into my former career and rebuilding my client base in the hair industry. My boss, Frank Prasek, welcomed me back with open arms, but being gone for three years meant that I was basically starting over again. Rebuilding was risky because of the economy in Houston and the fact that I worked 100% on commission. But I did it before, and I believed I would do it again.

I was willing to tackle this giant, but that meant that I had to work long hours, and the kids spent more time in daycare than with me. As many know, having dual careers often poses its own challenges, particularly with young couples, especially when they start a family. Eli and I had competing visions about my being a stay-at-home mom versus going back to rebuild my clientele at that time. I was able to balance the monetary costs associated with rebuilding my business (i.e., childcare, gasoline, supplies), but the family was out of balance.

You may find yourself in a similar situation, in the middle of a conflicting time with your spouse. It could be over something small or something gut-wrenching like deciding on the care for a terminally ill loved one or the best way to deal with a rebellious child. Each person has an opinion and a position to defend, and the conflict can fester into a full-blown storm. Because the marriage relationship is about more than just being right, it's crucial to avoid conflict and reduce tension as much as possible.

That conflict continued until the day I boxed with God in 1987. But God was gracious to me that day. When I accepted that the Lord wanted me to give up my desire to rebuild my business and trust and serve Him by serving my husband and children, I quit my job that day. Eli was surprised when I told him what I had done, but I assured him that the decision had nothing to do with what he or I wanted; it was God's decision. Although we had to adjust, Eli knew that God had spoken and had answered his prayers.

God told me to concentrate on being a good wife and a mother, which would keep the family steady, especially with the kids being so young and Eli being on a fast track in his corporate career. Eli called this strategy "anchor and float." In other words, one of us needed to anchor the family while the other floated to earn income for the entire family. I had no doubt regarding Eli's ability to hustle and provide for the family. He has an entrepreneurial mindset.

This is a more traditional lifestyle, one that both sets of our parents modeled in our growing up days. Anchoring is hard, and so is floating. This strategy requires teamwork and immense trust in God and each other. God never makes mistakes! Wouldn't you know it? Less than two years later, Eli's mad hustle landed him a promotion, moving us to Jacksonville, Florida. I would have had to quit anyway!

Living "happily ever after" is the marriage ideal for two uniquely created individuals who each have their own life dreams. Just like a boat, a family can be floating along just fine when a breakdown can occur due to a storm, an obstacle, or lack of fuel. Illness, financial loss, complicated family relationships, or a host of other hardships can also push you off course from where your dreams began, leaving you feeling discouraged.

A boat can drift miles off its course due to turbulent winds and strong currents. If the boat happens to turn broadside to the waves, it can be overcome by the waves and may even capsize. That's why every good ship has an anchor on board. An anchor is a tool used to connect a vessel to the bed of a body of water to prevent the boat from drifting away from its dock or from capsizing in a storm. While the vessel can still drift up to a point, the anchor keeps the boat fixed to its overall position.

In the same way, God told me to keep things steady, allowing Eli the latitude to float into the fog of his professional life, often taking him away from home and sometimes into uncharted territory while our family remained anchored. This approach helped Eli's stability as well. He floated into many storms as he worked multiple jobs simultaneously. But it was always rejuvenating for him to float back home to the kids and me, his anchor.

The anchor and float strategy may not work for everyone. It is submission—not to be confused with subservience, which is unquestioning obedience to your spouse. I remember an elderly woman telling me when I was about thirty-one years old that if my husband is saved, I am to serve the Savior in him. I know he's just a man, but I see the Savior in him. I totally submit myself to the will of God, which means I yield to God as the authority in my life. I am willing to humble myself to God's will and align my gifts with Eli's. He's an amazing provider, which makes it easy to support his ventures.

What would the anchor and float strategy look like in your personal relationship?

Too many people abandon the ship when the storms of life show up on the horizon. We all know God intended marriage to last a lifetime, but this doesn't always happen because of the storms that come. That's why it's crucial to make an irrevocable commitment to your marriage and work toward it every day. Eli and I call it "staying power." God told me on that day in 1987 that Eli and the kids were my new career. I listened, I learned, I grew organically, and I supported. I am blessed to have had the privilege to anchor our family.

At times, you have to refuse to let go. But here's an important point to remember you must each have a personal commitment to the marriage to make it work. If one person is following through and the other is not, then it will not work. If one person is anchoring the boat, but the other has already jumped off the boat, it will not work. Likewise, if both people want to be the anchor or both want to be the float, the marriage may not last.

A successful marriage only works when both people are fully committed to the process and the path that God lays out for them. I'm convinced that this strategy has propelled our marriage. So convinced, in fact, that I refer to anchor and float in the lyrics to my song "In a Ditch," which Eli included in the introduction to this book."

I agree with Fern and appreciate her sharing about the anchor and float strategy. Daring to believe is challenging and often more challenging in marriage. But when you're able to fully commit to each other and God, trusting that what He promised will come to pass, the rewards can be more than you could ever expected. Dare to believe.

By graduating and receiving my doctorate, I had achieved a huge goal in my life. But I wasn't done yet. In fact, looking back I can see that, in many ways, I was just starting out.

FIVE SMOOTH STONES

1. What would the anchor and float strategy look like in your personal relationship?
2. How has the giant called Waiting come against you in the past? Do you feel successful in the battle against him?
3. How does waiting on God make you feel?
4. Is there a pivotal decision you need to make—a dream you need to let go of?
5. What is it that God is calling you to dare to believe?

9

THE ACADEMIC ENTREPRENEUR

Thought-starter: In the Bible, what does James 2:26 mean by "faith without works is dead" (NKJV)? How have you adopted this concept into your life?

Just because I had finished my doctoral program did not mean it would be smooth sailing from here on out. There were still going to be giants to face. God was not finished with me. He continued to put me in situations that required me to engage my faith, dare to believe, and run toward my Goliaths.

After my third college graduation, I had the opportunity to stay close to home, joining the University of Houston faculty. I was happy to have the job, but it was a humbling position for me to take. It didn't matter that I had years of sales and sales management experience in the corporate world or had earned a doctorate from a prestigious university. Nope, I had to start over as an assistant professor just like everyone else on the faculty. I was now launching my third career, but, in many ways, I felt like I was back "on my knees," just as I was at the beginning of my time at Quaker Oats years ago.

So, I started at the University of Houston as an assistant professor. As I began, I was very keen to emulate my mentors, Dr. Paul Busch, Dr. Len Berry, and Dr. Steve McDaniel, who encouraged us to be excellent in all areas of academics. I remembered their examples of developing skills in all four areas: research, teaching, service, and administration.

PUBLISH OR PERISH

The first area I focused on was research. But research in an academic sense involves much more than just gathering and analyzing data. You're expected to publish your findings. In academia, you've got to publish to be academically qualified. There's an old saying in academia: "You've got to publish, or you'll perish."

Publishing helped me in my role as the dean of Mays Business School at Texas A&M. I was responsible for evaluating faculty members' research and teaching performance. I reviewed their research dossiers, read their articles, and sent the dossiers out for internal and external reviews before making the decision on whether to promote. These faculty members are promoted to associate professor and full professor—or not—based on this rigorous peer evaluation process of the research that they've published. Research at A&M is vital; it is a "tier one" research institution.

As an assistant professor on the tenure track at the University of Houston, I was required to publish peer-reviewed academic journal articles, which wasn't an easy feat to pull off. I was expected to publish in the best journals in marketing even though some of the top journal editors boasted that they had just a 7% acceptance rate. Yep, you read that right. There was a 93% chance that one's work would be rejected at a top journal!

Let me give you an idea of what publishing in peer-reviewed academic journals entails. I spend a great deal of time thinking about current events, existing research, and what needs to be done to advance research in sales, sales management, and strategy. I have spent my research career building off my time in the field as a salesperson and a sales manager and staying abreast of changes occurring in practice through my consulting work with companies. As a business dean, I was in constant contact with entrepreneurs and corporate businesspeople. I still am. So, I'm always learning and thinking about what research questions need to be addressed.

This premise gives me a starting place, a jumping-off point. So, I start digging. I collect data from organizations, companies, their salespeople, their sales managers, and their customers. Then I work with my coauthors, who are usually former doctoral students and dear colleagues. We go in and do a deep dive analysis of all the data we've collected. It's not odd to discover different outcomes with the different ways we run the analysis. That's what we do as academics. We make additional contributions to the body of knowledge that's already been published. As you can imagine, this process takes a tremendous amount of time and effort.

For every paper you see in publication, I can tell you it took countless hours to get it there. First, you've got to come up with a concept. Then you've got to do a lot of reading. You've got to collect and analyze the data. Then you write the paper, which is typically 40–50 pages with tables, figures, and references. Once you have the paper written, you're still not done. Now it must go through an extensive peer-review process.

This process is very involved and can take months, sometimes years, to complete. First, you send the article to a journal. The journal editor then reaches out to three to four professors from other universities, who are experts in the area that you're writing about, for a blind review process. In the intervening months, you check the email regularly, and finally, you hear back. Typically, it's a rejection letter. The editor tells you that regardless of all your hard work, "Sorry. This doesn't make much of a contribution. We reject the paper."

That kind of rejection is prevalent in my world. Very early on, I developed a thick skin, learning that if I wanted to succeed in the academic publishing world, I would have to learn to defeat the giant called Rejection.

In our doctoral student training, we train students to take those kinds of rejections and continue to write. It's a lot like sales. In sales, you deal with rejection all the time. But you must pick yourself up, dust yourself off, and get back out there. Getting your research published is the same way. You learn to fall back and regroup, go back in, and take a fresh look at the data and your analysis, then re-write the paper considering the reviewers' suggestions.

You rework, rewrite, and resubmit the work. Sometimes this process can go back and forth several times before you finally receive a positive response from the editor. "This is good. I like the kernel of your idea, and I can see where this research could contribute, but you still need to do a few more things." You may need to go back to the company to collect more data. You may need to do some reworking of your theory development and hypotheses, or you may need to try another statistical method. This is just a taste of the immense amount of work it takes to get just one article published. As an assistant professor, I was expected to spend at least 60% of my time in this research publication process and was expected to have several top-tier articles published in the six-year window of time on the tenure track.

> *What is your interpretation of the scripture, "faith without works is dead" (Jas. 2:26 NKJV)? In the Kingdom of God, the reward of work well done is not a day off, it's more work to do. In the parable, Jesus talked about the talents (Matt. 25:14–30). The only servant punished was the one who didn't try.*

TEACHING

So, 60% of my time was spent doing research, and about 30% of my time was meant to be spent teaching my students. But as you can probably guess, teaching involves a lot more than just standing in front of a class, talking to a group of students. There are lectures to write, lesson plans to develop, and tests to grade (or oversee teaching assistants who will help proctor and/or grade tests and check on homework assignments). I also had to maintain office hours that were supposed to be dedicated to helping students, not working on my latest writing project.

In my case, I had two sections of students to teach each semester, one section of 235 and another section of 250. So, I had close to 500 undergraduate students that I was personally responsible for as an assistant professor. A few years later in my career, I taught MBA students as well. You can bet that it was a lot to keep track of.

SERVICE

With 90% of my time taken up with research and teaching, 10% was reserved for any service responsibilities. Service is the third component for successful professors on the tenure track.

Because we were so busy with other things, the dean and department head usually didn't require a lot from the assistant professors in the way of service. A typical expectation was to bring guest speakers in to speak at one of our research seminar series.

While working on this task, I got the chance to meet and get to know Dr. Larry Chonko, who has since become a very dear colleague. It turns out that Larry is a graduate of the University of Houston's doctoral program in marketing who pursued sales research. At the time I met him, he was a full professor at Baylor. The service obligation I was supposed to do was to find a scholar in my research area and invite that person in to give a research talk to our faculty and doctoral students. I invited Larry Chonko. There's more to Larry's story, which I'll share with you later.

When was the last time you felt God stretching you so that you would be able to handle new responsibilities? Isn't it interesting that we are rarely ready for the promotion God wants to give us, but He promotes us anyway?

So, 60% of my time was spent doing research and writing peer-reviewed journal articles. I spent 30% teaching almost 500 students a semester and 10% doing work like inviting scholars to come in and speak at the research seminar series. But in true entrepreneurial fashion, I was looking for even more to do to advance the sales profession. In truth, I was fed up with people joining my profession and not doing things correctly.

I've learned to set high expectations, not only for myself but for my family and for those I work and serve with because I work to the glory of God, who has high standards. We must walk by faith and move in our calling, our purpose. We do so with bold confidence in Jesus as our Lord and Savior.

THE PROGRAM FOR EXCELLENCE IN SELLING AND SALES EXCELLENCE INSTITUTE

In addition to everything else I was doing, I was simultaneously working on an ambitious new venture, along with a team made up of adjunct professors and one retired executive professor. I was the only full-time academic/practitioner on the team and wasn't getting paid for this project, nor did I expect pay. I viewed it as my gift back to the sales profession.

My service responsibility should have been to simply find speakers for the seminars periodically, but I was doing way more than that! We called the venture that we worked on the Program for Excellence in Selling at the University of Houston. For me, it was truly an entrepreneurial effort and a labor of love.

You see, selling is much more than just a job for me. I love the profession of selling, and co-designing the sales program at the University of Houston was something I was compelled to do. I think selling is a noble calling.

I believe that properly trained salespeople are courageous revenue producers. They're good at solving problems, and so much about business, and life itself, is all about problem-solving. It's about critical thinking. It's about helping others.

During my corporate years, I got impatient with watching untrained or poorly trained college graduates go into my profession and mess it up, giving the profession a bad reputation. They tried being pushy, thinking that would earn them sales. They were manipulative and controlling.

Every time I saw this, I thought to myself, *No! That's not the right way to do it. Successful selling is about two things, repeat business and getting referrals. You want repeat business, and you want to get referrals. That's how you build a business!* In my experience, pushy and manipulative salespeople don't care much about the customer. They'll do whatever it takes to make the sale. If you're going to be pushy and manipulative, you might get the initial sale, but you're not going to get repeat business, and you probably won't get any referrals.

Once God stretches you, you will never go back to your original shape. What has been your experience in this stretching process?

Through my years of experience, I had learned a better way. For me, it was never about meeting a sales quota; I had more pressing concerns. *I was selling my way out of poverty.* If I didn't learn a better way to sell, I would not have been able to provide for my family. I knew that the best way to market was by being "customer-centric," putting the customer and her needs first, just like my time at *The Eagle* newspaper taught me. Now that I'd earned my Ph.D., I wanted to give back by teaching what I'd learned to a whole new generation of young salespeople. But it wouldn't be easy.

Not only was I not getting paid for this effort, but I wasn't getting any funding from the university either. It was like the old saying, "You've got to eat what you kill." I knew the program would be successful. We just had to figure out how to earn enough revenues to pay the expenses. I had to stretch my faith and dare to believe that God was in this venture. I was determined that we would succeed, so once again, I ran toward the giant. Actually, there were two giants: Uncertainty and Risk-taking. These giants were familiar to me. I watched my parents run toward these Goliaths multiple times.

Our team met to form our value proposition, which we outlined whenever we recruited companies to partner with us. We would ask them, "How much are you spending on training newly-minted salespeople, college graduates who want to join your company in sales and sales management? How much money are you spending just on the training and education?"

The answers we heard ranged anywhere from $75,000 to $200,000 a year per new hire. The $75,000 usually came from financial services companies. The $200,000 came from big, global companies, like pharmaceutical companies. We proposed working with these companies and providing them with a more efficient, more economical training model. In return, they would help us fund our program. We initially offered three different levels of participation—$10,000 a year, $25,000 a year, and $30,000 a year. We later raised the price to $50,000 and eventually offered a much more involved, strategic level that was $100,000, with a two-year commitment.

We told these companies, "If you provide the funding to us, we will help these college students understand the concepts of selling. We will role-play with them and take them to national collegiate sales competitions to test what they have learned in the program. We will get them ready to join your company. Your focus will be to give them the product knowledge that they'll need to be successful, and our focus will be to educate them in the art and science of selling, from the foundations of selling, advanced professional selling, customer relationship management, sales management, and key account selling." We later added a sales practicum, and in all courses, the students had to role play and did live selling. By 2007, the Sales Excellence Institute was generating just under $500,000 per year, the equivalent of approximately a $10 million endowment!

Our team put together a six-course sequence that students had to complete to receive a certificate in professional selling. The program has become one of the top sales institutes in the country, educating undergraduates and doctoral students.

As the program grew, we kept expanding our offerings. Talking to our corporate partners about research and executive education opened up more possibilities. We told them about our expanded program offerings, such as conducting research using data from their companies.

This strategy helped our doctoral students who were interested in sales and sales management issues. They were able to partner with faculty to analyze the data and write summaries of what we found in our study. This informed the decision makers in the partner companies. "In return, we will publish the findings in academic journals without revealing your company's name."

As a result of working so closely with the client companies, we were able to build deep relationships. They were not only getting sales talent from the undergraduate program, but they were also getting expert statistical analyses from the doctoral students, with the guidance of our faculty.

Today the program is called the Stephen Stagner Sales Excellence Institute, and in addition to educating young salespeople, it has become a go-to active pipeline for universities to hire doctoral graduates who are working in sales and sales management. So, partner companies get access to undergraduate and Ph.D. students.

I'm very proud to say that my youngest daughter Elicia is a graduate of the program. After graduating from the University of Houston with a marketing degree, a minor in sales (which was introduced the semester that she graduated), and a certificate from the Program for Excellence in Selling in 2005, she joined Cisco, which was one of the corporate partners that invested in the Program for Excellence in Selling.

With a tremendous amount of pride, I look back on those years building the Program for Excellence in Selling and the Sales Excellence Institute and the work we accomplished while I was at the University of Houston. There were plenty of times when things got tough, and I wasn't sure we'd be able to pull it off. But I knew it was the right thing to do, so I dared to believe that by the grace of God and the incredible talent of my team, we'd succeed. And we did, to a far greater extent than I ever thought possible.

After a decade of working hard to build the program, I became an associate dean in 2007 at the Bauer College of Business at the University of Houston, and not quite a year later, I was offered a job at Louisiana State University (LSU) to become the dean of the E. J. Ourso College of Business in Baton Rouge, Louisiana. Fern and I were empty nesters and ready for the next adventure that God had in store for us.

Set high expectations for yourself and dare to believe that God will give you the confidence to do His will.

MORE "CROSSROADS" INFLUENCERS

Over the years, God has been so faithful to bring just the right people into my life at just the right time, at critical crossroads. My years at the University of Houston were no different. God continued to be faithful to answer my prayers by bringing these vital influencers across my path. It's incredible to me how many times the answer to my prayer wasn't a thing or an event at all; it was a person showing up in my life at just the right time.

LARRY CHONKO

I first met Larry Chonko when I invited him to come to the University of Houston to be a guest speaker in our research seminar series. He did a great job discussing his research in sales and sales management. Through that experience, Larry and I got to know one another and found that we connected on several research ideas. Since that time, he's become a longtime friend and trusted colleague.

There was a time when I was developing a research idea that I knew I wanted to write about, so I reached out to Larry as a sounding board, someone to bounce my ideas off of. When I told him what I was thinking, he surprised me by saying, "I was just thinking about the same thing! Let's work together on the research project."

The two of us began to partner together on several projects culminating in a textbook that we published in 2005, *Selling ASAP: Art, Science, Agility, Performance*. We later published a professional edition of the book in 2012 for working adults. I have learned a great deal over a lifetime of selling everything from classified ads to consumer-packaged goods, and I wanted to share that learning in a book. Larry is someone that God put in my life at a critical moment to get my research career started.

CARL STEVENS

Another man that He sent at just the right time is the other coauthor of *Selling ASAP*, Carl Stevens. Carl worked very closely with Zig Ziglar, and lots of people involved in sales know of Zig Ziglar. At the time of writing this book, Carl is ninety-five years old.

It was an article in the *Houston Chronicle* that brought the two of us together. The newspaper sent a reporter to campus to do a feature story on the Program for Excellence in Selling that we were in the process of building. The reporter wrote about the field of sales and sales management and how the University of Houston was stepping up to prepare undergraduate students for a career in sales. They took a picture of me and two of my daughters—Elicia, who went through the sales program, and Tracia, our middle daughter, who graduated from the University of Houston and majored in psychology.

At the time, Carl was working for a lot of companies as a sales trainer. He's a true practitioner, while Larry is a true academic ... I'm a little of both, a hybrid of the two. That's why the three of us made such a strong team. Anyway, Carl had read the Houston Chronicle article, which also featured him and his long career in teaching sales and sales management to executives.

Carl reached out to me and said, "I really want to write a book with you. I think you bring in a fresh perspective." But the timing was terrible for me. I was on the tenure track at Houston, and my time was very limited. I was busy writing academic articles, and books don't count when one goes up for tenure and promotion in business.

Carl asked me, "How long is your tenure track?" I told him it's typically six years, and I'm in my fourth year. The tenure clock ticks loudly when assistant professors are trying to publish their research in the best journals while trying not to worry about whether they will do enough in the timeframe that the university allows.

Being the consummate salesperson, Carl asked, "You eat breakfast, right?" I laughed because I knew where he was going with the question. I told him that I do. He asked me, "How about we meet once a month and have breakfast together?" So that's what we did for about two years. Once a month, Carl and I would grab breakfast together and talk about sales and the sales profession, imagining if we were to write a book, what would go in it.

When I finally got close enough to go up for tenure and promotion to associate professor, we were able to start on the book. We published the *Selling ASAP* textbook two years before I was promoted to full professor.

Defining moments in life are almost always accompanied by defining people entering your life at just the right time. What are your defining moments? What are the names of the people who have impacted your life?

A POWERFUL PRAYER

My time at the University of Houston was a blessing. Those were years of tremendous growth and stretching for me. Looking back, I can see that this was just God preparing me for the next phase of my faith journey. God had much more in store for me than becoming a full professor. Little did I know that a simple prayer prayed out of a sincere heart could impact my life so much.

FIVE SMOOTH STONES

1. What is your interpretation of the scripture, "faith without works is dead" (Jas. 2:26 NKJV)? In the Kingdom of God, the reward of work well done is not a day off, it's more work to do. In the parable, Jesus talked about the talents (Matt. 25:14–30). The only servant punished was the one who didn't try.

2. When was the last time you felt God stretching you so that you would be able to handle new responsibilities? Isn't it interesting that we are rarely ready for the promotion God wants to give us, but He promotes us anyway?

3. Once God stretches you, you will never go back to your original shape. What has been your experience in this stretching process?

4. Defining moments in life are almost always accompanied by defining people entering your life at just the right time. What are your defining moments? What are the names of the people who have impacted your life?

5. Set high expectations for yourself and dare to believe that God will give you the confidence to do His will.

God is never finished with us. He has more for you and me that's a perfect fit.

10

A CUSTOM-MADE SUIT ... TO RUN IN

As David was preparing to fight Goliath, he said to Saul after he dressed David in his own tunic, "I cannot go in these ... because I am not used to them" (1 Sam. 17:39 NIV). So, he took the tunic and bronze helmet off.

Thought-starter: What do you do when you encounter a "now what" moment in your life?

ZIG ZIGLAR, MY HERO

One of my heroes in life has to be Zig Ziglar, the famous author and motivational speaker. But at his core, he was a salesperson. Something he said has become my favorite quote and a core value that I believe with all my heart: "You can have everything in life you want if you will just help enough other people get what they want." Isn't that amazing? The wisdom found in that quote is profound. If you only focus on what you really want in life, you'll rarely achieve it. You must instead focus on others and helping them get what they want.

For me, Ziglar's quote, from the first time I heard it, caused an awakening in me. I believed that what I was doing was so far beyond me, so much more than I could have done on my own, without God's help. In that context, it was easy for me to talk to others about stretching their faith, daring to believe. When I applied that principle to my own life, I was willing to believe that my tenure would be taken care of if I took my eyes off my wants and focused on helping people get what they wanted.

I was confident that if I focused on helping these students understand the discipline of selling and finding the courage to go out and do some remarkable things in business, God would take care of me. There was no need for me to stress out over this tenure clock. All I had to do was dare to believe in Him.

I prayed that He would also take care of my kids. He has been faithful every step of the way, answering my prayers in far greater ways than I ever imagined. In many ways, I feel like I'm living out Ephesians 3:20: "Now all glory to God, who is able, through his mighty power at work within us, to accomplish infinitely more than we might ask or think" (NLT).

As a result of God's abundant faithfulness, not only did I get tenure, I got it one year early! Remember, tenure is usually a six-year clock. But I was tenured in five years, and then five years after that, I became a full professor, which is the highest level and usually takes anywhere from twelve to twenty years to achieve. In fact, some people are lifetime associate professors, never making it to full professor. But I was fortunate to make it in record time. It was incredible. Because I believed that what Ziglar said was true, that if I focused on helping others, God would take care of me ... and He did.

I was so blessed to be able to meet Zig Ziglar before he passed on November 28, 2012. At the time, he was hosting a Monday morning prayer session with his entire staff each week. Early in 2008, I was invited to his offices in Dallas to lead the prayer in one of the prayer sessions. I was not only allowed to meet him, but I was also able to meet his whole staff. My son Chris, who was twenty-five at the time, came with me. It was such an incredible experience. I remember walking with Zig to and from the meeting. It was just the three of us, my son and me walking with the world-famous sales guru and one of my all-time heroes. What a memorable moment that was for me.

How does daring to believe relate to Zig Ziglar's quote: "You can have everything in life you want if you will just help enough other people get what they want"?

NOW WHAT?

We all know those times. Times when you've worked so hard to get to the top of the mountain. You've struggled through all the hardship, opposition, and exhaustion. You've finally gotten to the summit and achieved your goal. Standing back, breathing in the rarified air, and admiring the view. *Wow! I made it!* Then those feelings turn to a feeling that's almost anticlimactic, followed by another thought: *Now what?"*

For years, I had been on this arduous journey to earn my tenure, given up a lot and sacrificing deeply to achieve this calling. Now I'd made it. I did the research, published the articles, taught the classes, and graded the papers. I felt like I'd climbed all the problematic steps, from assistant professor to associate professor, *with tenure!* And I

> *I needed a new vision for my life.*

was well on my way to becoming a full professor. I felt like I'd scaled Mount Everest, and now, standing at the top, I wasn't sure what to do with myself. For so long, the possibility of tenure had kept me going. Now having achieved the goal, I wasn't sure what came next. I felt almost empty, aimless, and uncertain, which were new feelings to me.

In the last chapter, I shared with you the mantra in academia, "If you don't publish, you'll perish." Well, there's another saying about perishing, this one from the Bible. Proverbs 29:18 says, "Where there is no vision, the people perish" (KJV). In many ways, that's just the way I felt. I needed a new vision for my life. I knew God had called me to transform lives through education and teaching. But now, having earned three degrees and achieving tenure, I wasn't sure what came next. I was beginning to hear the corrosive whispers coming from the giant called Quest for Significance.

In the middle of a questioning time of introspection, I was wrestling with Significance, wanting to make a real impact and leave a legacy that would be truly meaningful. People who know me will tell you that I thrive on decisive movement and action. Just like my dad told me, "There's always something you could be doing."

I was still running the Program for Excellence in Selling, teaching, and writing but still wasn't content. I felt like I was wearing someone else's clothes. They were nice enough, but they weren't suitable for me. They just didn't fit right. I was looking for a custom-made suit, not something off the rack—one size fits all. In the meantime, I was traveling and presenting my research, which I enjoyed, but I sensed that God had more out there for me to do. I was not in my perfect rhythm.

How do you defeat the giant called Quest for Significance?

ANOTHER COMING FULL CIRCLE MOMENT

During this uncomfortable season of reflection, while still living in Houston, Fern and I regularly attended Lakewood Church. John Osteen passed in January 1999, and his son, Joel Osteen, had become our pastor. Lakewood moved in the summer of 2005 to the Greenway Plaza area in a building that used to be known as the Compaq Center. But back in the day, when I was a radio DJ in Houston for Majic 102, the building was known as the Summit. The sports arena became a very familiar place to me during those years. I attended many concerts and emceed a few in that very building. I vividly remember performers like Prince, Time, and Vanity 6 playing concerts there, with Vanity 6 performing their hit, "Nasty Girl." Now look at what God has done! That building, though remodeled, is now a place of praise music and worship! Yet another full-circle moment for me!

A SIMPLE PRAYER

In 2001, God led me through another crossroad, and just like before, He had placed just the right person at that spot in the road to help direct my steps. Lakewood Church hosted a seminar to which they'd invited an author to talk about his new book, which had become a bestseller. The name of the author is Bruce Wilkinson, and his book is *The Prayer of Jabez*, published in 2000.

Over several sessions that weekend, Bruce shared his story of writing that book. He also talked about the things that God taught him during the process of writing the book. He told us about God challenging him to pray the prayer that Jabez prayed in 1 Chronicles 4:10: "Oh, that you would bless me and enlarge my territory! Let your hand be with me, and keep me from harm so that I will be free from pain" (NIV).

For me, this was a defining moment. The crowd seemed to fade into the background, and it felt like Bruce was talking just to me. The seminar concluded in a final session through which Bruce encouraged us with the same challenge God had presented to him: to pray the prayer of Jabez. Never one to back down from a challenge, I took his words seriously. I could sense in my heart that God was daring me to believe that He would do what He promised. He'd answer my prayer if I could find the faith to pray it. I remember looking over at Fern, who was sitting next to me, and saying, "I should try it. I have nothing to lose."

Bruce shared with us about how hard it was at first to commit to God's challenge. If you think about it, that's a bold prayer to pray. It's one thing to read the story of Jabez, but it's quite another thing to muster your courage, run toward the giant, and pray the man's prayer. He makes some strong requests in the prayer. *Bless me. Enlarge my territory. Let your hand be with me. Keep me from harm. Keep me free from pain.*

But Bruce took up the challenge and prayed the prayer, not just once but over and over, every day. And God was faithful. He answered Bruce's prayer, and He began to do great things on his behalf. It was the perfect message at the perfect time for me—just what I needed to hear. I leaned over and told Fern, "I'm going to commit to that. I'm going to pray that prayer every day."

I walked into church that day asking, "What now?" and left with a new prayer on my lips. I had no idea what God would do, but I couldn't wait to find out. The first time I prayed the Prayer of Jabez was that day in my seat in church. I just bowed my head and prayed the prayer word for word, right from 1 Chronicles 4:10: "Oh, that you would bless me and enlarge my territory! Let your hand be with me and keep me from harm so that I will be free from pain" (NIV). I've continued to pray that prayer every day since.

*What is God challenging you with right now?
What is He daring you to believe?*

IS IT TIME FOR YOU?

Are you brave enough to pray that prayer? If you, like me, believe that God answers prayer, then this can be a scary prayer to pray, requiring lots of courage and a great deal of faith. You must have the willingness to *stretch* your faith. Like I mentioned before, this is a strong prayer, full of specific unconditional requests. I don't see where Jabez gives God an out by tacking on the phrase, "If it be your will." Nope. He's boldly taking God at His word, asking the big ask, and daring to believe that God will be faithful. Can you pray that prayer? Are you ready?

Let's pray together right now, slowly, deliberately, giving thought and emphasis to the words in bold.

> Oh, that you would **bless me**
> and **enlarge my territory**!
> Let your hand **be with me**
> and **keep me from harm**
> so that I will be **free from pain**. Amen!

Remember, the challenge isn't simply to pray the prayer one time; it's to repeat the prayer so many times that it becomes part of you, part of your very DNA, knit into your mind and heart. This wasn't easy for me. I was still filled with doubt, but just like working out builds your physical muscles, praying this prayer will build your faith muscles. You'll feel your faith begin to grow and deepen when you hear yourself pray this prayer every day and allow God to stretch you. You'll see God show up in your life in new and creative ways. That's what He did for me, and I'm certain He'll do it for you too if you're diligent to pray the prayer.

What's keeping you from taking up that challenge?

CONSISTENCY + TIME = RESULTS

Days turned into months and months into years as I continued what had become my daily practice of praying that prayer, doing what I could to remain faithful to the promise I'd made to God in that seminar at Lakewood Church. I knew that just like water steadily dripping on a stone, even the smallest of things done consistently over time could yield great results, and taking the time to pray is no small thing.

The prophet Daniel was faithful to pray consistently, to the extent that he'd built a public reputation as a man of prayer. Daniel 6:10 says, "Three times a day he got down on his knees and prayed, giving thanks to his God, just as he had done before" (NIV). There are few things in this life more potent than consistent prayer. James 5:16 says, "The earnest prayer of a righteous person has great power and produces wonderful results" (NLT).

I love that: "... *produces wonderful results.*" But notice, the wonderful results come as a result of what kind of prayer? Earnest prayer! Another translation uses the word "fervent." If you want to see results in your prayer life, you must be consistent, earnest, and fervent!

ENLARGING MY TERRITORY

Three years after committing myself to the practice of praying the prayer of Jabez daily, things began to happen. In 2004, I gave an academic talk, presenting one of my research papers in Vancouver, BC. There was a lady in the audience I barely noticed. I just figured she was another professor. Typically, audiences attending these talks tended to be primarily made up of professors. After my speech, she made her way down front for a chat with me. "Have you heard of Duke Corporate Education, Duke CE?"

I said, "I've heard of Duke University. Why?"

She said, "No, not Duke University. This is a separate entity. It's Duke Corporate Education. Our clients are the best-in-class companies around the world. We pick the best-in-class faculty members from top universities around the world to teach our client's executives."

I said, "Really? What does that have to do with me?"

She said, "We'd like to invite you to join our faculty network."

I was astounded, not sure I'd heard her right. I asked her, "Are you serious?"

She said, "Yes!"

Talk about an opportunity that fit me to a T! I had spent years early in my career as a successful corporate executive. On top of that, I had earned my Ph.D. in marketing, received tenure, and was on track to being promoted to full professor. Up to this point in my academic career, I had taught hundreds of undergraduate and graduate students in dozens of classes. I knew in my core that I was called to teach. Now here was an opportunity that brought those two worlds, worlds of which I was perfectly suited, together. God had given me a custom-made suit. This opportunity was not off the rack—not one size fits all. It was a tailor-made 48L!

I knew in an instant that this opportunity was an answer to the prayer I'd been praying. God was enlarging my territory. I agreed to join the Duke CE network, and that decision changed my life in ways I could hardly imagine. For the next several years, I worked with Duke Corporate Education, which was ranked number one in the world in executive education, according to the highly regarded business publication *Financial Times*, twelve years in a row. Number one in the world!

The very first client that we approached together was Cisco, the network solutions giant. We put together a proposal to teach the Cisco executives. We didn't get that one, but the next bid we landed was HSBC, the big global bank. To be given a chance to influence executives from a worldwide company was more than I could have dreamed, certainly more than I ever asked for. It was another Ephesians 3:20 moment for me. I was humbled and amazed by God's answer to my prayer.

It was unbelievable. There I was, part of the Duke CE Global Learning Network. Talk about playing to my strengths! I was a corporate executive, working for companies like these clients before becoming an academic, and now I came full circle, again! I was teaching corporate executives. I was in my sweet spot, not just teaching but teaching executives. Remember, we talked about finding your rhythm, finding your calling. For me, without a doubt, it was writing and teaching. But God narrowed it down even more, and as you'd expect, He was right on the money. I was doing the exact thing that ideally suited me—a custom-made suit. I ended up being able to teach around the world during my years with Duke Corporate Education. God was enlarging my territory.

I also picked up a teaching assignment at Vlerick-Leuven in Ghent, Belgium. There, I taught sales management to a group of master's students one week a year. When I traveled to Europe for the first time, I remember staying in the Ibis Hotel in Ghent, Belgium. I arrived after dark for my teaching assignment and went straight to bed, wanting to get a good night's sleep before teaching the next day. I woke up the following day and headed out of the hotel. On my walk to the university, I looked up to see an imposing medieval castle. I was blown away! Arriving in the dark the night before, I had completely missed this ancient treasure.

It was almost too much for me to take in. I am just a regular guy from Sunnyside, Texas, and later Somerville and Bryan, Texas, all tiny communities, and now I'm in Belgium on my way to teach master's students, who typically spoke four different languages: Dutch, French, German, and English. I walked out the front door of my hotel and found that I was right in front of a beautiful castle.

Talk about being surreal. I was standing there on a sidewalk in Belgium, looking at something that I never thought I would see in my entire life. Not only that, I was doing something that I love ... and getting paid for it. Unbelievable. Only God.

As a result of doing my best to be faithful, quietly praying the Jabez prayer, and daring to believe that God would be faithful to answer, I was sent worldwide, blessed with opportunities to teach in Belgium, France, Hong Kong, India, Malaysia, the United Kingdom, and other places. I could even take Fern along from time to time, and sometimes even her sister, Cindi, to share these incredible experiences with me. I was also able to bless my baby brother, Kirk, to trips to three of those countries. One beautiful memory from this time was treating my mom to a trip to Rome to see the Vatican. Growing up Catholic, Mom always dreamed of going. God provided a way for Fern and me to take her, and Jo Ann joined us. So, not only was I being blessed greatly, but my family was also being blessed! I even got a chance to play drums with the locals while in Bangalore, India.

Photo courtesy of Dr. Vikas Anand

Through it all, on every single adventure, I just kept thinking, *Bruce Wilkinson talked about the Prayer of Jabez and how powerful it is, and now I'm here, living out the fruit of the seeds that Bruce had sown into my life. It's just amazing!*

The Jabez prayer also kept me from harm as I traveled abroad, sometimes to areas where terrorism was prevalent.

Are you brave enough to pray the Prayer of Jabez? Are you ready to commit to praying it every day?

MORE EXPANSION ON THE HORIZON

There I was, still an associate professor at the University of Houston while managing my side gigs, teaching for Duke CE and

Vlerick (2004–2008). However, my voluntary work with the Program for Excellence in Selling and the Sales Excellence Institute was getting me noticed in some unlikely places. I started getting calls from universities about being a dean. The first one came from Cornell. They had a hotel and restaurant management school, and they were looking for a dean to head up that school. Cornell is in New York, a long way from Houston, but I was curious, and after talking with Fern, I decided to pursue the opportunity.

But I realized early on that I had no idea what I was doing. I had no clue what a dean really did. But I persevered and navigated my way through the nerve-wracking two-day interview process. Guess what? I came in second place! A full professor from Michigan edged me out. Crazy! I was just an associate professor at the time, a lower rank than a full professor. Plus, I was on the faculty at the University of Houston, not even in the same peer-class of schools as the University of Michigan.

> *The experience of just missing at Cornell, against all odds, was a clear indication to me that God was up to something.*

The experience of just missing at Cornell, against all odds, was a clear indication to me that God was up to something. Because of Cornell's interest, I was now considered a likely candidate for other schools looking for a dean, regardless of my current level of work experience. God was clearly working behind the scenes on my behalf.

And my phone began to ring. Other schools were calling. I was being pulled out of my comfort zone into so much more.

FIVE SMOOTH STONES

1. How does daring to believe relate to Zig Ziglar's quote: "You can have everything in life you want if you will just help enough other people get what they want"?

2. How do you defeat the giant called Quest for Significance?

3. Are you brave enough to pray the Prayer of Jabez? Are you ready to commit to praying it every day?

4. What is God challenging you with right now? What is He daring you to believe?

5. What's keeping you from taking up that challenge?

11

GOD'S STRETCHING PROCESS

Thought-starter: In what ways has God stretched you so you could fit into His bigger vision for your life?

Often the best way to see the hand of God moving in your life is by looking through the rear-view mirror. Sometimes we don't see or feel God working on our behalf until days or even years later when we look back over the path we've been traveling. Some years ago, a pastor taught me that God hears our prayers and begins orchestrating people, events, and things on our behalf to answer our prayers according to His will and the purpose that He has for us. He moves people and creates circumstances, and this all takes time. So far in this book, have you noticed the many people that God moved and the circumstances that He created for me to get blessed the way I have been?

Yes, I was diligent in praying the prayer of Jabez, and yes, I honestly wanted God to enlarge my territory. But by 2004, when I reflected on the last few years of my life, I could see that God was beginning to prepare me, daring me to believe for a bigger vision long before I'd ever heard of Bruce Wilkinson or his book. God wanted to do so much more in my life, but He had to stretch me first.

Today, I can see God's hand on my life, maturing me to believe in a bigger vision, which begun while we worked on the Program for Excellence in Selling at the University of Houston. The original design of it called for it to cater primarily to the technology industry, taking the students through a curriculum that would be highly sought after by technology companies in Houston. We'd already approached companies like BMC, Cisco, and a few others.

But I had the idea that the program could be so much more and should expand to include other industries. I thought, *Wait a minute, why are we restricting ourselves just to tech companies in the Houston area? Why don't we build the program in such a way that we would have a global presence? Why don't we dare to believe that we can create a program that would be known around the world? This program is good enough to appeal to many industries, including financial services and pharmaceutical companies.* I encouraged the co-director at the time, "Let's not restrict this initiative to just geography or industry. Let's dare to believe bigger! This is a bigger vision!" Later the program expanded to include a wide array of industries and business interests nationally.

> "Most people are afraid of their biggest ideas."

Of course, today, it is known worldwide, not just as a University of Houston offering but as the powerhouse, Program for Excellence and Selling, and later, its elevation to an institute that we named the Sales Excellence Institute. I even remember asking Fern to help me create a visual so that others in the program would better understand the bigger vision. We used an umbrella to show the team how the Sales Excellence Institute would encompass the Program for Excellence in Selling, plus academic research and executive education.

The truth is, much of the time, we're not guilty of thinking too big; we're guilty of thinking *too small*. In most cases, God has a much bigger vision in mind than we do. That was the truth that

He birthed in me about that program. He wanted me to stretch out my faith for a bigger vision. That's what daring to believe is all about.

Now, as I look back on those days, I can see where God began the stretching process years before He led me to pray the prayer that He would enlarge my territory. God definitely had a custom-made suit, made especially for me. But I was going to have to grow into it first.

God's stretching process had to begin in my mind before the first action could ever take place. He needed my mind to start thinking on a higher plane. Effective faith requires accompanying effort, but all actions begin in the mind. That's why God must change our thinking before He can change our behavior. Warren Barhorst, founder and chief executive officer of Iscential, an Aggie friend, and fellow author, says, "Most people are afraid of their biggest ideas."

The change in my thinking began with a random comment from an acquaintance who was a sales professor at Cornell. The words struck me like lightning out of a clear blue sky: "I want to nominate you for the deanship of the Cornell Hotel and Restaurant Management School." I was an associate professor and had no real idea of what a dean even does.

> *It changed the way I thought about myself!*

But before God could enlarge my territory, He had to broaden my thinking.

Suddenly, I was in a race involving a national search with three or four highly qualified candidates (each more qualified than I was) for the Hotel and Restaurant Management School at Cornell. And even though I didn't get the job, the nomination alone changed the way people thought about me. More importantly, *it changed the way I thought about myself!*

Because of the Cornell nomination, my name made it onto a list of some kind, which recruiters use, and the phone began to ring. Schools and recruiters were calling, and they weren't calling with faculty opportunities. They wanted me to consider being their dean. First, I was asked about a dean position at the University of Alabama, Birmingham (UAB). Then Michigan State called about their open dean position.

Finally, I got a call from an old friend, Dr. Rudy Hirschheim, who met me when we were on the faculty together at the University of Houston. He moved to Louisiana State University (LSU) and was serving on the search committee that was looking for a new business dean. He called me to tell me that he'd just recommended me to the other search committee members to fill the open position at the E. J. Ourso College of Business at LSU.

I was humbled by his belief in me for that position, but I couldn't help but wonder if I was cut out for a deanship. I knew I was a researcher and teacher at my core, and I loved my time in the classroom. I wasn't sure I wanted to make a move to administration. Maybe not getting the job at Cornell was a blessing in disguise. I shared my reservations with Rudy.

Later, I met another search committee member, Richard Matheny, a business lawyer who was serving on the LSU E. J. Ourso College of Business Dean's Advisory Council. He told me, "Eli, don't you see? Your impact on students will be so much greater as a dean than as a professor."

"How so?" I asked. "I have over 200 students that I currently interact with in the classroom and another 100 or so in the Program for Excellence in Selling. I'm also working on research with doctoral students. That's at least 300 lives per year. I'm already in a position of influence." Richard just shook his head.

"But as dean, you'd be in a position to impact thousands and not just the students. You'd influence faculty, other administrators, alumni, even donors. You would have a much larger impact." God was truly enlarging my territory.

*Before God can enlarge your territory,
He must enlarge your thinking.*

The light bulb finally went on. I knew I had been called to transform lives, and I had spent much of my adult life trying to hone my craft of selling, teaching, and leading to be a success. I'd climbed that mountain and made it to the top. But I still felt unfulfilled. That's because I was missing the bigger impact piece, one that could influence generations of young people, professor colleagues, staff, and donors.

I saw what Richard was trying to get across to me. Did I want to be a successful professor, or did I want to expand my influence and affect generations as a dean? I was beginning to sense that God was up to something—another crossroads moment. God had brought Rudy and Richard into my life at just the right moment to pivot my thinking from just working for short-term success to leaving a long-lasting legacy.

In a flash, I saw myself differently. My mind had expanded; I was a "dean candidate," and with that new revelation about myself, I took a hard look at each of the dean options. Ultimately, I chose to pursue the position at Michigan State in East Lansing and LSU in Baton Rouge.

What an unbelievable journey I was on! Since getting tenure, I had gone from being an associate professor to being considered for the dean's position at an Ivy League university. Just a few years later, I was promoted again at the University of Houston and became a full professor. Now I found myself simultaneously running for prestigious dean positions at Michigan State and LSU. It was almost too much to take in. But there was more stretching to come.

RUN TOWARD YOUR GOLIATHS

In what ways has God stretched you so that you could fit into His bigger vision for your life?

A GRUELING PROCESS

It's funny to think about now, but at the time, the interview process was grueling. I was expected to interview on both LSU and Michigan State campuses in person, which meant hotel rooms needed to be arranged and flights needed to be booked. Fortunately, Fern was in charge of logistics and moved me around wherever I needed to go. Over the years, Fern has been an incredible partner and anchor, always willing to help me with the logistical aspects of my job.

The interview process takes place over two consecutive days, with very few breaks. With almost no time to yourself, you're shuttled from place to place, always on the go and always "on stage." Every hour on the hour, you're meeting with a different group of people, some of who are closely watching every move you make and parsing every word you say.

It's like picking your way through a minefield, hoping you don't say or do the wrong thing. You're completely under the microscope every minute of those two days. From early morning breakfasts to late dinners, you're paraded past tables of delicious-looking food all day long. Still, every time you prepare to take a bite, someone important asks another probing question, meaning you hardly get to eat. This is fine because, amid all the stress, your appetite has dropped to zero. These interviews are grueling! Some meetings are one-to-hundreds, some are one-to-dozens, and a few are one-on-one meetings.

My first stop was Baton Rouge, where I interviewed at LSU. I'll have to admit, Fern and I both had much more of a comfort factor when we thought about the job in Louisiana. Not only did I know Rudy, who was on the search committee, but both Fern and I also have Louisiana roots. Remember, my dad was born in Louisiana. Fern's mom was born in Louisiana, too. We know the culture and its people, and we love the food. Also, my sister Jo Ann graduated from Dillard University in New Orleans. So, we know Louisiana, and we could easily see ourselves moving there then.

But I wasn't about to take the opportunity for granted. In preparation for the interview, I did a lot of research. I did my best to familiarize myself with key faces and names of people I'd likely meet. I even prepared a PowerPoint presentation that covered a little of my story and some of my core values, particularly as they pertain to higher education.

I survived the two-day process, but I couldn't relax yet. I had to jump on a plane and fly to East Lansing and do the whole thing all over again at Michigan State. More meetings, more new people to meet, and more faces to remember. After those two days, coming right on the heels of the two days in Baton Rouge, I felt like my smile was tattooed on my face. I could hear the giant named Exhaustion calling my name. But I couldn't rest yet. There was more work to do.

I had a previously scheduled executive education program with Duke CE in Hong Kong, China. So, even though I was finished with the LSU and Michigan State interviews, now I had to get to the airport for an international flight to Hong Kong. Fern and I had planned to use the trip to celebrate our wedding anniversary, and she was going to meet me at the San Francisco airport during a layover stop. The two of us hopped on a plane bound for Hong Kong. We even enjoyed a short stop in Taipei before continuing our journey.

Once we landed in Hong Kong, I had just one day to catch my breath and adjust my body clock before launching into five consecutive days of teaching executives. Needless to say, I had to be on my game, and with Hong Kong twelve hours ahead of us, I needed a reset. For me, night was day, and day was night, so I had to flip my body clock. Otherwise, I would feel like I was teaching a room full of high-powered executives in the middle of the night. Noon felt like midnight to my body.

Our wedding anniversary is on April 16, which just happened to fall on the last day of the executive teaching program. So, Fern had been preparing for us to spend some quality time together, seeing some of the local sights. But as the last teaching session wound down, I could feel the weariness beginning to set in. I was ready to fall in a heap and sleep for days.

After two days of interviewing at LSU, I've never been so tired in my life, two days of interviewing at Michigan State, hopping on an international flight, then standing on my feet in front of executives for five full days. What a nine-day run. I was utterly exhausted!

Meanwhile, Fern had our anniversary agenda ready to go, and she slipped into the back of the classroom just as I was beginning to close things out. I remember her looking so beautiful that it was hard for me to keep my concentration. I still think she was trying to distract me on purpose!

Our eyes met across the room, and with one look, she could tell how exhausted I was. She knew the anniversary plan was going to have to wait for another time. I felt so bad! There's nothing I wanted more than to spend time with my wife, but nothing was going to happen until I got some rest! We finally rested and took a couple of days to look around Hong Kong before flying back home.

Does God ever give a bigger vision than you can handle?

OVERWHELMED

It had been just a few short years since I committed to pray Jabez's prayer daily. I remember feeling like my life had significantly accelerated as God was expanding my mind as well as my territory. I was being stretched mightily to fill the custom-made suit He had prepared just for me. I was filled, even to overflowing, and I was worn out.

As much as I loved the prayer of Jabez, I wasn't sure if I could handle much more expansion. I felt like changing my prayer from "Lord, expand my territory" to "Lord, it's too much! Slow down a little, and let me catch up!" I later added "and expand my resources" to the prayer.

I was utterly overwhelmed. I remember one day, as weariness settled on my shoulders like a heavy wet blanket, my sister-in-law, Cindi, was staying with us. She's always had a sympathetic listening ear, so I unburdened myself and unloaded the heavy weight I'd been carrying around the past months.

I told her about my busy schedule, full of obligations. I told her about God stretching me, feeling pulled this way and that. I told her about my increasingly busy travel schedule and all the well-meaning folks vying for my time and attention. I even confided to her how conflicted I felt. I mean, God was answering my prayers in such a genuine and abundant way. Was I ungrateful by being so worn out by it all? Finally, I broke down, "Sis! I'm overwhelmed. It's just too much!"

She just smiled in her knowing way and said, "Brother, you've got to stop relying on your own energy and start relying on God's energy." Now you must understand, there's no one better to say something like that to me than Cindi. She has enormous battles of her own, giants that she has to face every single day. In 2001, just about the time I started to pray Jabez's prayer, Cindi's health began to decline, suffering from one disease after another. She's been battling bravely for the last twenty years. She truly is a miracle walking, and she knows all about relying on God's energy.

When she told me that I needed to rely on God's energy instead of my own, you can bet I took her words to heart. Not only do I love and respect her because she is family, but I also knew she was living out those words every single day, fighting her giants. She had earned the right to speak into my life in this particular area.

God was expanding my territory, to be sure, but He was developing me too. He was stretching me so I could handle the increased capacity He was putting on me. I was confident that my purpose in life was no longer just success; it was legacy. And God was asking me if I was ready to influence generations. In my heart, the answer was a resounding YES!

> *Much of the time, we're not guilty of thinking too big; we're guilty of thinking too small.*

So I stood upright, squared my shoulders, and faced the giant called Exhaustion. I ran toward the battlefront with the words of the apostle Paul on my lips: "I can do all things through Christ who strengthens me" (Phil. 4:13 NKJV).

STORM CLOUDS AHEAD

As the Michigan State/LSU decision loomed, Rudy Hirschheim, my friend on the LSU search committee, and his wife, Sally, visited Fern and me, coming to our home for a face-to-face meeting. He assured me, "Eli, this is a real search. For the last ten years, we've been trying to build a business education complex for the business school, and we just can't seem to wrap it up. We need a sales guy to come in and help us close this deal. We need you. If you're looking for legacy, this is it."

At LSU, the business and engineering schools were sharing space in the same building, Patrick F. Taylor Hall. For the previous ten years, they'd been trying to raise money to build a separate building, a whole new complex, just for the business school. Getting that complex built intrigued me. I had some fundraising experience getting companies to partner with the Program for Excellence in Selling, but I had not secured any major gifts. However, I am a salesperson, and the challenge appealed to me.

So, in March 2008, I agreed to become the dean of the E. J. Ourso College of Business at LSU. Little did I know that storm clouds were gathering on the horizon. Just when I felt that I was breaking through the feelings of being overwhelmed, the inky black shadow of the giant called Death fell across my path, threatening to overtake me.

THE GIANT CALLED DEATH

Once I decided to accept the dean's position at LSU, Fern and I planned our move to Baton Rouge, and the excitement came. In many ways, it felt like we were striking out on our own. Our four kids were grown, we were empty nesters, and we were both ready to float together, moving farther away from our home base than we'd ever lived before. In many ways, this job would be a completely different experience for us, but we were up for the new adventure!

I'll never forget the day—June 28, 2008. It was a Saturday. Fern and I were in the process of getting settled into our new condo in Baton Rouge, unpacking boxes, and getting furniture arranged.

I got a call about five o'clock that afternoon from a man who introduced himself as a police officer. He asked me, "Are you, Eli Jones?" I told him I was. I was immediately on high alert, thinking, *This can't be good.*

The officer said, "Sir, your dad was involved in a fatal accident." The only thing I processed was the words "your dad" and "fatal." Of course, I knew what the word fatal meant but was having trouble connecting the dots.

Out of shock, I asked him, "Are you telling me that my dad is dead?"

He said, "Yes, sir. It was a car accident." My dad was 86 years old at the time, but he was still relatively healthy and strong. We never dreamed he'd die in a car accident.

My dad and mom had sold their farm, and they were in the process of building their new home. He was at the new place, which was nearing completion. Evidently, he was pulling out of the driveway and was T-boned by another car barreling down the street. The giant called Death, which some say is the most fearsome giant of all, had just stepped into my life.

In a daze, I thanked the officer for the call, and I hung up the phone. I was in shock. I looked at Fern and said, "We've got to go home. We've got to go now." I wasn't even thinking about the funeral, so I didn't even pack a dark suit, no dress clothes of any kind. We just quickly grabbed whatever we thought we'd need, just a couple of sets of clothes each, and we took off driving. We were going from Baton Rouge, Louisiana, back to Somerville, Texas, which is where my mom and dad lived at the time.

Along the way, I was entirely led by God. I've never read an instruction manual on what to do in these situations, so I was operating on autopilot, just doing the next thing next. I was only days away from starting my new job in a completely new role, and the folks at LSU were expecting me to hit the ground running. Now my dad's death had thrown all that into question. I knew I had to call the university provost, my new boss.

I got her on the phone and told her, "My dad just died, and I've got to go home."

She was very kind and said, "We'll move your start date. You go ahead and take care of what you need to take care of."

So, Fern and I were in the car driving from Baton Rouge to Somerville, about a six-and-a-half-hour drive. We were both on our phones the whole way, trying to get the news out to family and friends. But I had yet to make the most important and difficult call, the one to my mom.

I knew that I had to notify my mom of what just happened to her husband, my dad, but I was dreading making that call. I finally mustered my courage and got her on the cell phone. It turns out she was in Bryan, Texas, which is only about a twenty-mile drive from where they were building their new home. My mom had her caregiver with her, and they were in the car in the grocery store parking lot.

Not knowing the right words to say, I began with some small talk while I figured out how to break the devastating news. I said, "Mom, how are you?"

She said, "Baby, I'm doing fine. How are you doing?"

In a flash of heaven's inspiration, I asked, "Do you have your nurse right there with you?"

She said, "Yes, she's here."

"Good," I said, "Would you put her on the phone?"

When the caregiver got on the line, I told her, "I've got some really bad information to pass on to my mother, and I need you to do me a favor. In a few minutes, I'm going to ask you to hand the phone back to her, and I'm going to give her the bad news. Then I want her to give the phone back to you, and I want you to grab my momma. I want you to hold her, hug her tightly, and let her know that her family is coming. We're all on our way." The nurse agreed to help and handed the phone to my momma.

It was such an unbelievably difficult situation to find myself in. What am I supposed to say? How am I supposed to tell my momma that her lifelong love was gone? They had been married for more than sixty years! I felt so helpless. The giant called Death was roaring in my head.

I took a deep breath to quiet the noise and said, "Mom, I've got to give you some really bad news. Dad was in a fatal accident."

My mom was in shock, and there was a long period of silence on the other end of the phone. I said again, "Momma, Dad is gone. Fern and I are in the car right now heading your way. We're about four or five hours away. Now hand the phone back to the nurse. Here's what I want you to do. Just listen to her. She's going to hold you now, but I want you to know that we're all coming. We're coming to be with you. We're on our way, and we'll be there as soon as we can." When the caregiver got back on the line, I said, "Do not take my momma to the accident scene. No matter what she says to you, do not take her there."

We buried my dad, and I was honored to eulogize him at the funeral service. Believe me, I had no trouble finding the words to say about my hero. Through many tears, I told the folks the story of "one spot at a time" and other lessons he'd passed on to me throughout his long life. It was a bittersweet day, so sad to say goodbye but so good to share precious memories from his life with family and friends. By the way, I later learned from my mom that the police officer called me at the accident scene by simply hitting redial on my dad's cell phone. I was the last one that my dad called.

I had no time to dwell on grief over the loss. I knew my dad loved the Lord and was in a much better place, so I had to shift my focus to fulfilling my duties as the new dean of the E. J. Ourso College of Business at LSU. I kept thinking, getting back to work was what my dad would expect me to do, given his work ethic.

What is the difference between success and legacy?

A DIFFERENT TYPE OF LEADERSHIP

The new job turned out to be a pressure cooker. I didn't know what I was doing half the time, and it's not like there's a dean school I could have attended, so I had to learn on the job. I was now leading faculty and had responsibility for the students and the staff. I was running on empty but dared to believe that I could do this job. I knew that God had directed me toward this job, and I was confident that He would give me everything I needed to get the job done.

I may not have known much about the dean's role, but one thing I did know: being a dean is all about vision and leadership, and leadership is something I had learned a great deal about while in industry. I just had to remember the leadership lessons from all those years ago in my corporate life.

The problem was, from the time I got the LSU job, I could easily discern that the leadership model is different in the academic world than it is in the corporate world. The last real leadership position I'd had was with Frito-Lay, but that model would need to be adapted. In academia, leading tenured faculty members, who are more like partners in a law firm or an accounting firm than they are employees, requires a different style of leadership.

Adapting my leadership style did present a learning curve for me, but nothing like the job of raising millions of dollars in the middle of a global financial crisis. The job before me was to raise $60 million to build a brand-new beautiful business education complex on campus. Bobby Jindal was the governor of Louisiana at that time, and the state had already committed to paying half of our goal since we were the flagship business school in Louisiana.

A GIANT CALLED INTIMIDATION

Even though I knew that they had pledges for $13.8 million of the $60 million projected for the project, raising the rest of the money loomed like a huge giant in front of me—a giant called Intimidation. The financial crisis had come out of left field, and the unexpected nature of it intimidated me. I'd forgotten the wise words of my dad, who always counseled me: "Son, you've got to be prepared for the unexpected."

No one really expected a financial crisis of that magnitude. It's like launching off into a plan you know is sound, but then something comes along that you didn't anticipate, throwing everything into disarray. COVID-19 is an excellent recent example. We were all rushing ahead, busy with our lives, and then the pandemic hit, something completely unexpected. Intimidation, Fear, and Worry all came taunting. You're left wondering what else might be out there waiting to bite you in the backside. For us, 2008 had become the year of the unexpected, first with my dad's passing and now with the global financial crisis.

A GIFT GIVEN ... THEN TAKEN BACK

I had just taken the dean's position and starting to wrap my head around what the fundraising for this new business education complex was going to look like when one of the board members called me up and said, "Hey, I've got a great prospective donor for us to meet with. I've been talking to him, and he wants to meet with you, have lunch and talk about the business education complex and your vision for the business school. Are you available?"

I told him, "Yes! Absolutely, I'm available."

I'll never forget that meeting. We're sitting at lunch. It's the prospective donor, the board member, and I. The donor had already heard the pitch from the board member, but now he wanted to hear from me. *What's the vision? What is this business education complex going to do? Why build it? What problems will it solve?*

So, there I was, sitting at the table in front of this guy and the board member. We'd done our research and confirmed that the donor was indeed a qualified prospect. He had the means to give a substantial gift. I'll bet we spent about two hours talking about the business education complex and what it would mean for the students, faculty, and staff. We talked about how it would help recruit and retain the faculty and ultimately elevate the reputation of LSU and the E. J. Ourso College of Business. Finally, the guy got up from the table, having finished his lunch. He looked at me, and he looked at my board member, and he said, "Okay. Put me down for two million dollars. I'll do it!"

What an amazing experience that was! In all my previous years in sales, success was always about exchanging money for something tangible. Whether it was a product or service didn't matter, as long as the buyer received some kind of direct benefit. But this was different. Donors aren't like buyers; they make their decisions based on a whole different set of motivations. Donors aren't expecting an exchange of goods or services or any other kind of direct benefit from their gift. That's what distinguishes fundraising or "friend-raising" from sales. Donors are not purchasing your product. They are "purchasing" your passion, your ideas, your vision, and they want to make a significant impact, leaving a legacy.

I walked out of the restaurant that day on Cloud Nine. I remember thinking, *I never knew fundraising would be this easy!* My first shot at securing a major gift out of the gate, and I closed a donation of $2 million!

Then came the unexpected. The global financial crisis hit hard, and the donor had to retract his donation. The big gift was there ... and then it was gone.

For the next four years, the fundraising part of the job was hard, very, very hard. The giants, Overwhelm and Intimidation, were constantly trying to overtake me. This was a whole new territory for me, and I felt entirely out of my element. God had big plans for me, and He was stretching me to meet the new capacity. This was a big stretch for me—a considerable stretch. I was out of my comfort zone. Thank God things did happen, and by His grace, we met our fundraising goal, but let me assure you that there were plenty of "dare to believe" moments all along the way, miracles for sure.

On my watch at LSU, from 2008 to 2012, we were able to pull off the building project even during a global financial crisis. Today, the LSU Business Education Complex is a reality, and all the credit goes to God. It took some arduous work from the whole team to raise the necessary funds, and in 2010, we broke ground. After two years of construction, we had a ribbon-cutting ceremony in 2012 with Steve Forbes delivering the keynote address.

But I would never have an office in that building. God was stretching me again, and this time He required unquestioning obedience.

FIVE SMOOTH STONES

1. In what ways has God stretched you so that you could fit into His bigger vision for your life?
2. Does God ever give a bigger vision than you can handle?
3. What is the difference between success and legacy?
4. Before God can enlarge your territory, He must enlarge your thinking.
5. Much of the time, we're not guilty of thinking too big; we're guilty of thinking *too small*.

12

A GIANT STEP OF OBEDIENCE

Thought-starter: Has God ever asked you to do something that didn't make sense at the time? If so, did you obey Him?

In 2008, Fern and I moved to Baton Rouge, Louisiana, for me to be the dean of the E. J. Ourso College of Business at Louisiana State University (LSU). While the work was difficult, I could feel the favor of God on us, and Fern and I were both convinced that we were right where God wanted us to be.

Soon after arriving in Baton Rouge, Fern got an exciting phone call from our youngest daughter Elicia, who had joined Cisco Systems in 2005. She got married the following year to Ryan, and they moved to Albany, New York.

On the call, Elicia told Fern, "Mom, Ryan, and I are ready to move back to the South. We're starting to think about having a family and feel that it's important for us to be close to them. We're not sure how it's all going to work out yet, but we know we're heading south."

Fern didn't hesitate to make a deal with our daughter (I'm not the only salesperson in the family!). Eager to get our baby girl just as close as possible, Fern told Elicia, "If you guys move to

Baton Rouge, I'll watch your baby for the first year while you and Ryan are working."

Fern's offer sealed the deal, and in June 2009, Elicia and Ryan had their first baby, Ean Hunter, and moved to Baton Rouge soon after, one full year after my dad passed. Having the family with us was great. They only lived about ten minutes away and, because Fern was keeping Ean, we got to see them every day.

Life in Baton Rouge was good. Sure, the job had its challenges, but personally, life was good. Our other kids were only about four hours away in Houston, so we saw our family regularly. Everything was rolling along just fine. But that was all about to change.

UPSETTING THE APPLE CART

In late 2011, just a couple of years after Elicia and her family moved to Baton Rouge, the Walton College of Business at the University of Arkansas started reaching out, asking me to think about interviewing for the dean's position.

At that time, I had only been to Arkansas one other time in my entire life, and I didn't know much about the state at all. So, I turned them down … several times. "No, thank you. There's just no way that we're going to move from Baton Rouge right now." I explained, "Our youngest daughter and her family are here with us. The rest of our family is close by, in Houston, and can drive to get to us in a reasonable amount of time. So, no, thank you. I'm not interested."

But they persisted, eventually calling me maybe five times. "We still want you to think about coming and interviewing for the deanship in the Walton College of Business." So finally, after about the fifth time, I talked to Fern about it just to gauge her interest.

Her reply was short and sweet: "No! We're not going to Arkansas!"

IT'S JUST A LOOK

About that time, I had a faculty member at the E. J. Ourso College of Business at LSU who had graduated from the University of Arkansas. She popped into my office one day after hearing through the grapevine that Arkansas was calling me.

She said, "Eli, you really do need to go look. Have you ever been there before?"

"Only one time," I replied, "and I didn't see much."

She said, "It's right in the middle of the Ozark Mountains in Northwest, Arkansas. It's beautiful." I already knew that Northwest Arkansas was the land of Walmart, J.B. Hunt, and Tyson Foods, three fantastic entrepreneurs who built a whole ecosystem in that area of the state. She continued, "You should at least go take a look at the opportunity."

By the time I'd gotten home from the office that evening, I'd about talked myself into making the trip to Fayetteville just to see what they had to offer. I told Fern, "I want to go. It's just a look. I want to hear what they have to say."

Fern said, "You can go if you want, but I'm not moving to Arkansas." Still not convinced, she said, "You're going to be there all by yourself if you decide to take that job." So, I went to the interview by myself. And the faculty member was right, it is beautiful, and the job was a fantastic opportunity.

The interview was a grueling process, just like the others had been. Two full days of meetings, every hour lined up with a new group of people eager to ask me questions. As it turned out, I was the fourth candidate in the search. The very last meeting I had was with the chancellor, Dr. G. David Gearhart. The meeting took place in the Chancellor's home on campus. He was gracious and very complimentary, and after several minutes of small talk, he looked at me and said, "Eli, you're our guy. We want you to be the next dean of the Walton College of Business."

I said, "Sir, I thank you so much, but I have to tell you right now that my wife is not on board with the idea of my taking this position. We've got family close by, there in Baton Rouge, and my wife watches our grandson and granddaughter so our daughter and her husband can work full-time. There's just no way we're coming to Arkansas."

Well, Dr. Gearhart wasn't about to give up without playing his highest card. He said, "You know what, Eli? I'm going to fly the university airplane to Baton Rouge on Friday to pick you up." (It was Tuesday at the time.) He said, "I'll have the plane there to meet you, and you can bring as many family members as you want to come and see Northwest Arkansas." Clearly, I had met another great salesperson!

I was stunned. I'd never had anything like that happen to me before. I'd heard of college coaches being flown in on university planes during their recruiting process but never candidates for dean positions. I was challenged, and all I could do at the moment was to accept his offer. And on the way back home, one thought kept rolling around in my mind: *How in the world am I going to persuade Fern to come see this place?* I called my sister Jo Ann to get some advice while in the airport waiting for my flight back to Baton Rouge.

As it turned out, I had some help convincing Fern to make the trip. Her sister Cindi talked with her and encouraged her to go. Cindi even drove from her home in Galveston, Texas, to Baton Rouge so she could make the trip with us. Lo and behold, that Friday morning, the University of Arkansas plane was right there in Baton Rouge to pick us up. And Fern decided to come along. We also took Elicia's two kids, Ean and Rylee.

So, there we were on the tarmac, Fern and I, the two grandkids, Ean and Rylee, and my sister-in-law, Cindi. We all hopped on the airplane and flew to Northwest Arkansas, trying unsuccessfully to pretend that this was all just an everyday occurrence for us! Yes, we were flying on a private airplane. It was an incredible experience, and I felt God was continuing to answer the prayer I'd been praying. He was enlarging my territory. It was just truly amazing, and the welcome party when we arrived was unbelievable. They had all kinds of people waiting to greet us.

We had such a great time. The university put on the full-court press as they shuttled us from place to place, showing us the sights and trying to convince me to take the job (I don't think it was any secret that the one who really needed convincing was Fern!). We got to tour the campus and surrounding areas and meet lots of genuinely wonderful people.

But the thing that sticks out most in my mind about that trip was our time at lunch. Dr. Gearhart had planned for us to meet and have lunch with Jim Walton, Sam Walton's youngest son. I'll never forget walking in and seeing Jim Walton sitting patiently at the table waiting for us.

Of course, Sam Walton, Jim's dad, is legendary, especially there in Northwest Arkansas. Jim was on the advisory board at the University of Arkansas. He's such a humble and modest man. His demeanor reminded me of what I had always heard about his dad: quiet, unassuming, and modest.

Anyway, we walked in, and there's Jim Walton, the chancellor, and the provost. I walked in with my wife, our two grandkids, and my sister-in-law. Chancellor Gearhart invited us to have a seat and graciously introduced us around the table. I was in awe. I couldn't believe it was happening. I almost wanted to pinch myself a couple of times, thinking this couldn't be real.

Gradually, as we ate our lunch, we warmed up and had some good, easy-going conversation. When we had finished eating, the chancellor looked at the provost and said, "Let's leave and give Eli and Jim a chance to talk." Everyone, except for Jim Walton and me, took their cue and got up and left the table, leaving just the two of us sitting there. That's when things got awkwardly quiet.

JUST THE RIGHT WORDS

There I was, one-on-one with Jim Walton. Jim is a quiet man by nature, and since I didn't know what to say, the table fell silent. Finally, God gave me something to say.

The way I know it came from God is because it just flowed so naturally. I know that if it were all me, it would have seemed forced and out of place. I looked at Jim and broke the silence by saying, "I want you to understand that I know what it's like to have a father who's your hero."

I'll never forget the look that I got from him. He turned toward me, and he stared for just a few seconds, but to me it felt like a whole five minutes! He smiled, and I could tell by that look on his face that he knew exactly what I was talking about. We shared similar feelings for our dads. That was an incredible moment for me, that connection to Jim Walton.

At that moment, I reflected on my dad. I wrote earlier about how my dad was an accomplished entrepreneur. Growing up, I had a front-row seat, watching him launch three separate businesses. My dad may not have built a retailing empire as Sam Walton did, but to me, my dad was just as successful.

FROM 0 TO 60

We had a wonderful visit to Arkansas. Fern and I, the grandkids, and Cindi were all blown away by the experience. Everyone was so welcoming to us. I was genuinely swayed by the hospitality and was just about ready to sign on the dotted line, but I knew that Fern was the one who needed convincing. Had the folks in Arkansas done enough to sway her vote? In the plane, on the way home, I tried to read her face and pick up any signals, but she had her shield up.

Finally, I couldn't wait any longer. "Fern, on a scale of 0 to 100%, with 100% being 'Absolutely, let's go to Arkansas,' and 0% being 'No, I'm not going!' Where are you on that scale?"

She looked at me and said, "Probably about 60% in favor." My mouth fell open.

I said, "Are you serious? 60% in favor of moving to Arkansas?" I looked over at Cindi, and I could tell she felt the same way. We all felt it. We knew there was something special there, something about those people and about that place. Something was going to happen there. But only God knew what.

When we got back to Baton Rouge, one of the first things I did was to meet with the LSU chancellor. I told him, "Look, I just want to let you know that I'm not looking to leave LSU, but I've been talking to the folks at the University of Arkansas, and it looks like they're going to make me an offer."

I continued, "I don't want you to counter their offer. I want to be clear that I'm not just using the this offer to try to get a raise from you." I honestly said that, and I meant it. "If I do leave LSU for Arkansas, it would be for something that I believe God is calling me to do. To me, this opportunity is all about being obedient to God." It truly was.

I did end up getting an offer from the University of Arkansas. And despite my urging, LSU countered the offer, and they matched Arkansas dollar for dollar. So, the way things stood, I could stay in Baton Rouge and get a nice raise in salary, be close to family, and move into the building I had worked so hard to raise money for. To sweeten the deal, LSU also offered me the title of associate vice-chancellor. I could expand my influence and begin to work on economic development for the state with the governor and the secretary of state, with whom I'd developed a good working relationship over the last few years.

Arkansas included in their offer an endowed chair. In fact, it's the largest in the country, the Sam Walton Leadership Chair. The choice seemed clear, but I was conflicted. How could I leave my team at LSU, especially after completing the Business Education Complex? Most importantly, how could I leave my grandkids, my daughter, and her husband? Also, Fayetteville, Arkansas, is much farther away from Houston, where the rest of our kids live, than Baton Rouge. How could I pick up and leave all that behind?

Ultimately, I knew the decision wasn't about me. It wasn't about money or titles or endowed chairs, or even about family. This decision was all about God and where He wanted Fern and me to live. It was time to be still and quiet and listen for His voice and what He wanted me to do.

Do you know what God's voice sounds like? Can you recognize when He's talking to you?

EARLY MORNING CONFIRMATION

It was early on the day of the deadline for me to decide whether I would accept or decline the offer from Arkansas. It was four o'clock in the morning, and I remember that I could hardly sleep, tossing and turning, wrestling with the decision. I finally got up and went in and stood at the kitchen island.

I put the offer from Arkansas on the bar of the island, and next to it, I put the counteroffer from LSU, and I started to pray. My prayer was all about asking the Lord to guide me. I felt the heavy weight on my shoulder, the pressure to make the right decision. With one hand on one offer letter and the other hand on the other offer letter, I cried out to the Lord, "I'm going to surrender to you, Lord. Guide me. Give me discernment. Help me see what I can't see right now. Help me understand what this is all about. I didn't ask for it, but the opportunity is here, and I know it's of you. Please help me."

I prayed and prayed. I don't know exactly how long I was there, but after a while, Cindi woke up and came in and joined me in prayer. She put her hand on my shoulder. A little while later, Fern woke up. She came in and joined us, putting her hand on my other shoulder.

All three of us were praying fervently over these two letters, asking for wisdom, knowledge, understanding, insight, favor, and discernment. "Lord, guide us. Tell us what you want us to do here." Suddenly, my knees buckled, and I looked over at Fern. At that moment, I had a sense of what God wanted us to do.

It's not that I heard Him; there was no audible voice, no bright lights, or descending angels singing the Hallelujah Chorus. Just a peaceful knowing came over me, the weight lifted from my shoulders, and I knew what we were supposed to do.

I looked over to Fern and said, "We are going to Arkansas. God wants us to go to Arkansas."

I looked over at Cindi, and she said, "That's validation."

Along with Fern, they said, "We feel the same way. We're going to Arkansas!" Though I knew the decision, I didn't know all that was waiting for me on the other side. This decision didn't make any sense, and I didn't know what it would mean for us.

Later that day, I called the provost at the University of Arkansas, and I said, "Well, I'm coming."

She said, "Really?" I could tell she was surprised. But now that I had made the decision, I had to do the difficult thing and walk it out. It wasn't as easy as simply walking away from LSU. I had a ribbon to cut, a new building to dedicate, and lots of people to thank, people who would probably not understand why I was leaving.

I remember the ribbon-cutting ceremony for the new Business Education Complex was scheduled to be on March 2, 2012. We had a big celebration planned. The governor would be there as well as many other dignitaries. Plus, I had asked Steve Forbes to come and formally dedicate the building.

Photo courtesy of the E. J. Ourso College of Business

The problem was that I had accepted the Arkansas position at the end of February. I was doing all I could to keep the press out of it. I didn't want the news of my leaving to break before the ribbon-cutting, before I had had the chance to thank the donors, the governor, and everyone else responsible for helping to make the business education complex a reality.

Well, just like Job in the Bible, what I greatly feared came upon me. The news leaked out and made things awkward for my final days at LSU. But in the end, the faculty and the staff moved right on into the brand-new Business Education Complex. My associate dean became the interim dean (and later the dean), and life went on as Fern and I prepared to uproot our lives and move to Arkansas.

Just because you're obedient to God doesn't mean it will all be smooth sailing.

HARD CONVERSATIONS

As difficult and awkward as it was for me to leave my job at LSU, it paled in comparison to the arduous task of telling Elicia and her kids that we were moving away. We'd been a consistent presence in their lives and telling them that we would be moving was almost more than I could bear.

I was walking around in the backyard with my little grandson, Ean Hunter. I was searching for just the right words to try to explain to this precious two-year-old that his Mema and Papa would be leaving. It was an excruciating experience, and it about ripped my heart out. That was so hard—probably the most challenging part of all—explaining to our little grandson that we were going away. Our baby granddaughter, Rylee, was too young at the time to understand what was going on, but our leaving was going to impact Ean's life for sure. Also, at this time, we learned that Tracia, our middle daughter, was pregnant with twins. Tracia and her husband lived about four hours away, in Houston. So, the timing of our move seemed horrible.

While in Baton Rouge, we were able to spend lots of quality time with family. But moving nine to ten hours drive time away to Fayetteville, Arkansas, would make that kind of frequent contact impossible. It just made no sense at all. Why would we ever pull out and go to a place that we didn't know? Sure, we had a great welcome on our visit, but the fact was, we didn't know the people there.

Why would we leave our youngest daughter and her family after they moved all the way to Baton Rouge for the sole purpose of being close to us? Telling my daughter was another very difficult conversation I had to endure. Elicia was hurt. She came to me and said, "Daddy, I feel like you're abandoning us. We moved here because of you and mom. And now that you're leaving, I feel abandoned."

HEARTBREAK

The giant called Heartbreak attacked with all his might. Not only did my decision to move break the hearts of people that I dearly loved, but the decision was breaking my own heart as well. I was at a loss for words. Nothing I said was going to take the pain away. I tried to explain that it was a spiritual decision, fully aware of how little sense it made in the natural.

Have you ever prayed for things, and God answered, but it was not anywhere close to what you wanted? That's what we were dealing with. My daughters were trying to understand it, but it just didn't make any sense. Fortunately, they are believers and have the capacity to comprehend spiritual things. I asked them to trust me, to trust God. I knew that the way to defeat the giant called Heartbreak was to put my trust in God, so I picked up that smooth stone and ran toward Goliath.

Proverbs 3:5–6 says, "Trust in the Lord with all your heart and lean not on your own understanding; in all your ways submit to him, and he will make your paths straight" (NIV). What an awesome promise that is. If we're faithful to trust in Him and not in our perception of how things should be, not relying on our own strength, then He will make our paths straight. If we remain submitted to Him, we can dare to believe that God will be true to His word.

I knew it was God. But I almost felt like Abraham when God asked him to sacrifice his only son Isaac. It made no sense. Why would God ask him to sacrifice his son—his son of promise? But Abraham was obedient anyway, not knowing how God would work things out, but he chose to trust, nonetheless. With me, I knew that God had upped the ante and was requiring *a whole new level of trust* from Fern and me. The question was, did we have the faith to believe Him? Would we obey Him and move to Arkansas, even though it was hard, or would we shrink back, make the easy choice, and stay put?

I took courage in something my dear friend and mentor Dr. Paul Busch once told me: "Most of the best things that have happened in my life scared me to death ... at first." I knew God was calling us to a walk of obedience, and I was determined to trust Him.

The Bible says to obey is better than sacrifice. But what do you do when God requires both obedience and sacrifice?

I remember that day in the backyard with little Ean. Holding his hand, I looked up to the sky and cried out to the Lord, "God, obedience shouldn't be this hard!" Not to be overly dramatic, but I mean, I was about to walk away from my precious grandson, and the pain in my heart was indescribable.

As much as I love my own kids, there's something very special about the relationship between a grandfather and his grandkids. Ask any grandpa, and he'll tell you this is true. Fern wrote about the precious spirit of the grandfather in her song from 2014.

"Spirit of the Grandfather"

A love so pure, so deep, so real ... he just cannot
  break away.
The moment he embraced the child, he exhaled old
  pain away.

For the child, he is a refuge
And a safe release
For him, a second chance in life
And where all judgment ceased

The most precious encounter
A treasure chest of love.
It's in the Spirit of the Grandfather
where you'll find the heart of God.

He knows there's no one else on earth ... with
whom the child feels free
You'll find them walking hand in hand while talking candidly.

To the child, he's so much greater than the man can see
For him, the reason why he strives to fulfill his legacy.

The day will come when he's no longer here—the child now grown but clearly hears ...
His words as if he were standing right there.

He said, "In everything you encounter, look only for the good."
It's in this spirit of the grandfather where you'll find the heart of God.

I love that line. It's so true: "It's in this spirit of the grandfather where you'll find the heart of God." There's just something so precious, so sacred about my relationship with all my grandkids. To think about walking away and leaving them was tearing me apart.

I didn't know what the ultimate mission would be in Arkansas and making such a monumental move without knowing why was very difficult for a planner like me. I focused on not leaning on my own understanding, daring to believe that God was leading, that everything would be okay.

In the end, Fern and I made a move to Fayetteville, Arkansas, and as we were settling into our new home, we walked upstairs and looked out the window at our new backyard, which looked bare and empty. The weight of our decision had settled on us. We had just moved the farthest that we've ever been from our family. I looked over and said, "This is either the best decision we've ever made or the worst. I really don't know which way this is going to go, but I appreciate you for believing in this move with me." I committed to Fern, telling her, "One way or another, we're going to see our grandkids as much as we possibly can."

Together we committed to seeing them at least once a month, and for the whole three years we were in Arkansas, we found a way to make that happen. We were always able to work it out somehow, some way. Sometimes we flew them on Southwest Airlines to Tulsa and drove two hours to pick them up, or we used airline points to fly them on United. Sometimes we drove, or Tracia drove the ten hours or so with a van full of grandkids to visit us. One way or another, we made it happen. We weren't about to lose the relationships we'd worked so hard to build with our kids and grandkids.

I wanted to tell that story because of the amazing way God was faithful to make good on His promises. Looking back, our short time in Arkansas was a nurturing time of growth, a time for us to rest and prepare for the next step in our journey. As we continued to walk into the unknown, floating in the fog, God was so loving, so encouraging, giving us little indicators, like breadcrumbs, telling us we were on the right path.

Can you truly trust your own understanding of a situation? What's the alternative?

YOU ARE THE ANSWER TO SOMEONE'S PRAYER

God used Dr. Matthew Waller to give me the first clue as to why He wanted us in Northwest Arkansas. At the time, Matt was one of six department chairs reporting directly to me. Just starting out, as a part of my process, I decided to meet with each department chair, one on one, off-campus. I asked each one a series of questions to gauge what they were going through.

I'd ask, "What are your plans for your department? What are you trying to accomplish? And what are some of your biggest challenges?" Asking these types of questions helped me get to know my team better. I made a point of doing this kind of thing whenever I took over a new team.

It came time for me to meet with Matt Waller. This would have been my second or third time being with him. I knew Matt to be a strong believer in Christ and was looking forward to our time together. We met, and I pulled out my little sheet of questions I was asking each department chair and prepared to take notes of his responses. I got ready to ask my first question, and Matt looked at me very sincerely and said with a big smile, "We've been praying for you."

I remember being confused by his comment, *Lord, I don't even know why we're in Arkansas. I don't know what this is all about, and now this guy says I'm the answer to their prayers? I don't get it.* I looked up at him and stared at him for a second before simply turning over my sheet of paper and saying, "Let's talk about *that*! I want to hear more!"

Matt began to tell me about all the believers there at the Walton College of Business and in the community, and how they had been praying for a Christian business dean. He went on to tell me about why that's so important to the culture of the place and how fervently they had been praying. In my mind, I'm thinking, *God, is that what this move has all been about? I've been feeling a tug from your Spirit, nudging us, pulling us, from Baton Rouge to*

Arkansas. Is this what that's been about? Are Fern and I the answer to their prayers?

I began to hear about this whole new movement of strong Christians in Northwest Arkansas. At the time, Mike Duke was the CEO of Wal-Mart. He is a strong Christian. His wife, Susan Duke, reached out and became good friends with Fern. Then I met Doug McMillon, also with Wal-Mart and the current CEO, and his wife, Shelley. We met John Roberts, who is the CEO of JB Hunt, and his wife, Tamara. Then Donnie Smith, the CEO of Tyson Foods at the time, and his wife, Terry. We became friends with James Barnett, CEO of DaySpring Cards, and his wife, Marilyn. These are all Christian men running huge organizations right out of Northwest Arkansas. We joined a great church and got to be friends with Mickey and Denise Rapier. We also became friends with Orson and Karen Weems, and John and Elizabeth English. God made a way for me to build community and to pray regularly with those believers.

> *When you're faithful to be obedient, God will give you much.*

LOOKING AT ARKANSAS THROUGH THE REAR-VIEW MIRROR

Like I mentioned in the last chapter, sometimes it's easier to see God in the rear-view mirror. That's particularly true here, as I look back at our time in Arkansas. I see His hand working His will with the very guy who met with me for lunch at the beginning of a very confusing time for me, the guy who said, "We've been praying for a Christian business dean." This is the guy I promoted to be an associate dean working alongside me and the person the university named dean of the Walton College when I left—Matt Waller.

I fundamentally believe that God used me to go there to work with Matt, for him to see what being a dean is like. Over the course of my three years as dean, Matt and I had many conversations. Little did I know that perhaps God moved me to Arkansas to work with Matt and inspire him to become a dean. Who knows?

Maybe God moved us to Arkansas to meet and get to know Al Bell? Fern already told you how monumental and life-changing our relationship with Al Bell has been for us. It was while living in Arkansas that we met Al, who has a home in Little Rock. Is that why God required us to make the difficult move? Who knows?

Can you think of an example from your own life when God was easier to see in the rear-view mirror?

As I look in the rear-view mirror at our time in Arkansas, there are just so many blessings that emerged during those three years, blessings that have filled us up. There were men from all over Northwest Arkansas who came to campus, came to my office right during business hours, and prayed over me. For two days, a steady stream of men came from all over Northwest Arkansas just to pray over me.

Photo Courtesy of Dr. Matt Waller

Our time in Arkansas taught me an important lesson about God's kingdom. When you're faithful to be obedient, God will give you much. When you dare to believe, to put your complete faith in Him, God will come through even when it doesn't seem to make sense. He'll do something amazing on your behalf.

We are able now to share that powerful story with so many people. That was a faith journey like none other we've ever had. We now know that when you are called to do a thing, and you obey, even when it doesn't make any sense, God will bless you beyond anything you've ever imagined.

After a wonderful three years in Arkansas, God had another surprising blessing lined up for us.

FIVE SMOOTH STONES

1. Do you know what God's voice sounds like? Can you recognize when He's talking to you?

2. The Bible says to obey is better than sacrifice. But what do you do when God requires both obedience and sacrifice?

3. Can you truly trust your own understanding of a situation? What's the alternative?

4. Can you think of an example from your own life when God was easier to see in the rear-view mirror?

5. Just because you're obedient to God doesn't mean it will all be smooth sailing.

13

GOING HOME

Thought-starter: Why does it so often seem that God's timing is different from our own?

LORD, SO SOON?

I'll never forget the phone call. It was a Sunday afternoon, and Fern and I had just returned home from church. I was looking forward to putting on some comfortable clothes and relaxing for a bit before getting a little weekend work done.

The phone rang, and on the line was my friend Paul Busch checking on Fern and me. He mentioned the dean search at Mays Business School at Texas A&M. He was calling to see if I had any interest in the position. My mouth dropped open. Talk about an opportunity coming out of left field! A&M was the place where I had earned all three of my degrees. Going home to A&M was an option I had never allowed myself to hope for. It was too wonderful for me even to consider.

I stammered a response, "Y-you mean I could have the chance to come back to my alma mater and lead the school from which I graduated?" That was precisely what he was suggesting. How incredible was that?

It was a Wow! moment, for sure, but the emotion that kept washing over me was, "Lord, so soon?" As initially difficult as the move to Arkansas had been, it felt like we were finally settling in. We had figured out how to continue to get quality family time with our kids and grandkids, and we were enjoying living in Northwest Arkansas. To leave Arkansas now after just three years, even for an opportunity at A&M, just felt a little off.

I remember talking to Fern about it, and she agreed that the timing wasn't good, but she also saw this as a tremendous opportunity to get back closer to our babies. I said to her, "This is our chance to go home. We've got to catch this train home!" So that's what we did; I agreed to throw my hat in the ring and become a candidate for the dean of Mays Business School at Texas A&M.

One of the first people I went to for counsel was Jim Walton, who had become a real support to me during my time at Arkansas. He was very, very helpful as I worked my way through this transition. When I told him about the opportunity at A&M, he said to me, "Eli, obviously we want you to stay, and if it were just any other university coming to call, we would most certainly be prepared to counter their offer. But we understand that A&M is home for you, and it's your alma mater. It's also about family, and you and Fern would be much closer to your kids and grandkids. So, we're not going to try to stop you from going home."

CONTINUAL COVERING IN PRAYER

As I mentioned in the last chapter, the blind faith journey from LSU to Arkansas was difficult for both Fern and me. God required a "next level" amount of obedience from us. He knew how difficult it would be and graciously surrounded us with a caring, loving, and praying community of believers there in Arkansas. From the time we arrived in Fayetteville, these dear people simply held us in their arms, both figuratively and literally. Spiritually and emotionally, we were fed there. Looking back, it's easy to see that going to Arkansas was our opportunity to pull up to the filling station and get full again.

Now, with the encouragement from both Fern and Jim Walton, I went through the interview process for the position at A&M. Once again, it was grueling, but this was home for me. I knew many of those with whom I was interviewing, and the process wasn't nearly as stressful as interviewing at a school that I didn't know well.

During my campus visit at A&M, I gave a speech to about 400 people. I titled it "Respecting the Past; Writing the Future." It became my "campaign platform," so to speak, as I encouraged my colleagues to view my deanship in that way. We would honor the long-held traditions at A&M while simultaneously working toward envisioning the future of higher education and moving our college toward it.

They extended an offer, and in March of 2015, I accepted the position, and we moved back to Bryan/College Station in June. I could hardly believe it. I was going back to the same business school that I graduated from. What an incredible and rare opportunity to be an alumnus of the business school and then be called back to lead it.

You attend college as a student, and you have teachers and professors leading you, coaching you, guiding you. Then, you get to go back to that same school as the dean, and now, the roles are reversed. You're the leader, the coach, the guide. What an honor that was. It was incredibly humbling for me to be in a position of authority over people I respected and had looked up to for many years.

Jim Walton was right. Going back to A&M was like going home to family, which is great but not without its challenges. On the one hand, it's like, "This is incredible. We get to go home. We get to be around for birthdays, anniversaries, holidays, and other significant events." But on the other hand, having family and so many very close friends close by kept us extremely busy. It seemed like every week, there were events we had to miss just because we had already committed to something else.

A lot of people were pulling us in a lot of different directions. It seemed like everybody wanted a piece of the Aggie son and his wife who had returned home. There were some familiar faces in the hallways and offices, by the way, people like Paul Busch, Len Berry, and Dr. Mac. Many of the marketing faculty members were still around from my time there as a doctoral student. What a fantastic welcome home for us. But I was feeling the effects of the constant demands on my time, professionally and personally.

We couldn't have been back for more than just a couple of months, and I felt like I had run ten laps around the track already. Being the dean of Mays Business School is such a demanding job by itself, but combined with all the other obligations, pulling and tugging me in different directions, it was almost more than I could handle. I thought back, again, to my sister-in-law Cindi's advice to operate on God's energy.

The word eventually got out to our family and friends, and they began to circle Fern and me in prayer and loving support. Their caring touched us deeply. And just like in Arkansas, God kept filling us up, surrounding us with a loving community. But here in Texas, it wasn't just business leaders who were reaching out in prayer; it was students as well. Our friend and my dear colleague, Dr. Ben Welch, organized a group of students and faculty to come to my new office and pray over me. Two Dean's Advisory Board members and dear friends, Jerry Cox and Willie Langston, drove from Houston to come to my office on campus and pray over me. My office was full of Aggies, and they were all praying for me. Talk about a 12th Man experience! The 12th Man is always in the stands waiting to be called upon if needed.

I found myself humbled by their love, their caring, and their prayers. But I knew that my security and peace weren't found in a room full of supportive friends, as comforting as that felt at the time. No, in the midst of that blessing of love, I was reminded that God and God alone is my safe place, my place of peace, assurance, and security.

It's hard for me to describe what it felt like being prayed for by so many precious people, but Fern has written a song that captures the feeling that she and I have when we seek peace, assurance, and safety.

"My Safe Place"

I put my head on your chest, and I can feel your heart beating
I feel the rhythm, and the cares of my soul start melting
You are my safe place, I rest in your embrace

On your lap, cradled in your arms, I'm sheltered from all harm
Why do we look for love in man, just to have our hearts broken?
God proved His perfect love when He sacrificed His only son
You are my safe place, and I no longer feel disgraced.

On the cross, you erased sin from me, your greatest gift of love is life eternally
I take refuge in the shelter of your wings, my strong and mighty tower, praises will I sing

So I have my head on your chest, and I hear your heart beating
And I feel the rhythm, and the cares of my soul are melting
You are my safe place, until the day I see your face
I'm on your lap, cradled in your arms, sheltered from all harm.

Even as I read through those words, I can feel God's peace fall on me. He, and He alone, is my safe place! God knew how much Fern and I were going to need that love and assurance in the coming days.

At first, the timing of coming back home from Arkansas to A&M seemed off to Fern and me, but as I look back in the rearview mirror, I can see just how perfect the timing was. God needed us back home, close to family. We moved back in June of 2015. In July, my eighty-six-year-old mom was diagnosed with breast cancer. By late September, she had gone home to be with the Lord.

Only God knows the future. Nothing is a surprise to Him. He knew all those dates and everything that was going to happen. He knew that He had to get us home to Texas to be near family, to be near my mom in her final days. Never forget, just because you can't see the reason for something God is doing in your life doesn't mean there isn't a reason.

How do you feel when someone says, "Just because you can't see the reason for something God is doing in your life doesn't mean there isn't one"? Does hearing this help you? If not, why not?

SAYING GOODBYE TO MOM

Like I said, I got to Texas in June of 2015. By late July, my mom had been diagnosed with breast cancer. I remember those months being crazy busy. Not only was I just beginning the new dean position, trying to meet all my obligations there, but I was also doing my best to help pick up the slack, helping my siblings care for our mom.

My sisters and brother, who were mostly retired by then, had been on the front lines caring for mom. They were taking turns watching mom, taking her back and forth for radiation treatment, and everything else that comes with being a cancer patient. At the time, I had to juggle many meetings at work, hopping in to help with my mom as much as I could. I was in a near-constant state of distraction. Whenever I was at work, I thought I should be with my mom, and when I was with my mom, I felt I should be at work. Probably the best example of this happened at the worst possible time, right at the very end of my mother's life.

As the new dean, I wanted to be sure and connect with many people that summer, primarily donors. Like at LSU, a big part of my new job at A&M was raising money, which required a lot more than just writing letters. "Friend raising," as I call it, requires authentic relationship building, making friends. And you can't do an effective job of that by phone or email. You need to meet face to face, look people in the eye, and share with them your vision for the college.

One day my sister Jo Ann called me and said, "Eli, Mom's caregiver called. Mom is not feeling well, and she needs to be taken to the hospital. I'm on my way, but it's going to take me a while to get there."

I immediately told her, "Okay, I'll head that way now." So, I cleared my schedule, jumped in my car, and drove to see my momma in the new house that my dad had been building when he died pulling out of the driveway.

When Jo Ann and I got there, we found Mom sitting at the edge of the bed, rocking back and forth, with her caregiver standing next to her. I said, "Momma, we're going to take you to the hospital." So, I gently lifted her and put her in the car. We drove her to the hospital in Bryan, Texas.

One of the most precious gifts that I ever received from God was something my mom told me that day. I was picking her up out of the wheelchair and putting her on the hospital bed when she whispered in my left ear, "Baby, I'm so glad you're home." What a confirmation that we'd made the right decision in coming home! If I ever doubted God's leading, my mother's words set me straight. The giant called Uncertainty was silenced once and for all. I was confident that I was exactly where I needed to be. This was why we were called back home.

We went through the process of getting mom admitted to the hospital. But it didn't take long for the doctors to determine that they had done just about all they could do for her. It was clear that it was time to move her into hospice.

CALLED AWAY

So, my siblings and I all gathered around her hospital bed, the four of us. My momma then went one by one, looking at each of us in the eye and simply saying, "Peace." That's the last word we heard our mom speak.

But even during this incredibly intimate family time, the job began to tug me away. The development officers at A&M had set up some visits, which were actually sales calls, in Austin and San Antonio. I tried to put them off, doing my best to spend as much time as possible with my momma. It was becoming clear that she was in her transition time, slowly passing away.

I was busy canceling appointments left and right, telling folks, "I'm not going to be able to make it. My mom is dying, and I'm going to stay here with her."

One of the development officers finally called and told me, "I understand that you need to cancel a lot of these appointments, but there's one that you really need to go to. It's extremely important."

I said, "My mom's dying. I'm with my family. We're in the hospital, and my mom is going to hospice."

He said, "I know, but this guy is a pretty big deal in Austin, and he knows a lot of really good people. I just don't think you should cancel this one."

I finally relented and agreed to go to Austin, but I warned him, "This better be extremely important."

Meanwhile, we moved my mom into hospice, putting her back in the house my dad had built for her. All my siblings were there in the house with her. We were going through the grieving process together, watching our mother gradually slip away.

This just happened to be the same night that I had agreed to go to Austin to speak to a group of potential donors. The development officer was going to meet me at my mom's house so I could spend just a few moments with her before going to the reception in Austin.

He and I walked into the house, and of course, I was suited up because I was going to the donor meeting. My family looked at me, saw how I was dressed, and sensed something was up, asking me, "Where are you going?"

I said, "I'm so sorry. I've got to go do this thing tonight." I gave my colleague a quick glance and walked into my mom's bedroom while he stayed in the other room with my family.

My mom was in bed, and I laid down right next to her and took in some deep, slow breaths. I softly said, "Momma, I've got to go do this meeting. I'm so sorry, but I will be back. Don't leave. I'll be back." And I left the room and got in the car with the development officer, telling him, "Look, I've agreed to do this reception, but you're going to need to get me there and back just as fast as possible."

Have you ever found yourself in a situation in which you've got to do your job, but you've got something personal and serious going on at the same time? How did you handle it?

Now, Austin is almost two hours away, and you can bet we got there just as fast as the law allowed. Before getting out of the car, I turned to my colleague and said, "Once I'm finished, don't forget to get me out of there as fast as possible. I need you to get me back to my momma just as soon as you can. Do you understand that?"

He said, "Yes, sir."

We walked into the house, and the host welcomed me. The house was full of people that he and his wife had invited. These were several of the most influential people in the state. I dove in, working the room, walking through, greeting folks, and thanking them for coming. Meanwhile, the development officer made his way over to the host and told him, "Eli has to leave pretty quickly after he talks. His mom is dying, and we've got to leave as soon as possible."

Stepping into that room full of people, I had to switch from "grieving son" to "college dean" in the time it took to greet the first guest and shake a hand. People were coming up to me, saying, "So, you're the new dean of Mays Business School. It's great to meet you." With a smile on my face but a pain in my heart, I did my best.

"Great to meet you, too."

After the meet and greet, the host finally said, "Everybody, let's go out by the pool. Eli's going to give us his vision for the future of Mays Business School." In the meantime, my mind was entirely on my mom, not on that group of potential donors. The host continued, "We're just delighted to have Eli back home at A&M. Eli, would you please say a few words?"

I got up and did my best to be upbeat. I told everyone there all about the vision of Mays Business School. I explained why I believe the school is excellent and some of the exciting plans we had for the future. I was engaging and cheerful on the outside, but on the inside, I was in agony, missing my mom, praying that she would still be there when I got back.

I wrapped up my presentation and immediately started to figure out how to get out of there graciously. But people surrounded me and shook my hand, saying, "It was so great meeting you. I really enjoyed talking with you. I wish you all the best."

I looked over at the development officer, saying with my eyes, "Get me out of here!" Eventually, we worked our way out of the house, jumped in the car, and sped back to my mom's house. I don't think I said a single word the whole way back. I can't even describe how I felt. There were so many mixed emotions.

We finally made it back about 11:00 that night, and I rushed into the house to see my mom. I went straight back to her bedroom, and I laid down on the bed, right next to her like before. I could see the gentle rise and fall of her chest; she was breathing. She hadn't gone yet! I took some more deep breaths. I said, "Momma, I'm back. Thank you. I love you." I got up from her bed and went outside to talk with Jo Ann. Just about five minutes later, my niece came outside, telling us, "She's gone. Meme is gone!" It was thirty-eight minutes after I had returned ... thirty-eight minutes!

To think that my mom passed just five minutes after I walked out of that room amazes me. I am so blessed that my mom held on to life while I had to go to Austin to give an inspirational speech. She held on until I could make it back. At some level, she understood that I had a job to do. I had to give a speech about why people should invest in Mays Business School: because it's moving, its trajectory is strong, and we're going to continue to grow and impact lives for the better. Meanwhile, my mom was back at home, dying.

If that's not running toward the giant, I don't know what is! Have you ever found yourself in a similar situation? A situation in which you're expected to perform a task, but you've got a seriously personal thing going on simultaneously. You've got to be able to compartmentalize and say to yourself, "That task is so important, but I've got to go do this now." That's where I found myself on that terrible night—pulled in two directions at the same time. But God was so faithful to me, and by His grace, He gave me strength. He helped me compartmentalize and slide one thing to the back burner while something else took center stage.

I take solace in knowing that my mom is in heaven. Back in Arkansas one morning, I sat next to my mom at the kitchen table, and I was led to ask her if she had made Jesus her Lord and Savior. I knew that she did by her actions and the way she spoke, but mom and I never really talked about it until that moment. As the sun lit her face through the shutters, I grabbed my Bible and prayed over her. I said, "Momma, I want to know for sure, and I want to be able to say to my siblings with certainty that you're in heaven."

She said, "Yes! He is my Lord and Savior."

How have you coped with the giant called Death? What do you say to others to encourage them during this experience?

SELLING A&M

Like I mentioned before, a good deal of a college dean's job is raising money for his or her college. In academia, we all might like to think we spend all our time researching and educating but traveling "on the trail" raising money will always be part of the job.

To give you an idea of the enormity of these campaigns, as I write this, Texas A&M is closing out a $4 billion capital campaign. You read that right. That's $4 billion, with a B! We ended up raising $4.2 billion overall. It was a total team effort, and we all worked very hard to achieve that goal.

At Mays Business School, our goal was to raise $139 million over the campaign's timeframe, which was a stretch goal for the school. Praise God we were successful, raising about $205 million. Working closely with the development team and raising that kind of money was extremely challenging but, at the same time, extremely rewarding. It was an amazing journey.

But I did much more than just raise money. Like my dad taught me, "There's always more you can do." I stayed busy leading my team of faculty and staff, and I still made time to write and publish academic research.

COMING HOME TO CONNECTION

Coming home to A&M has been such a full-circle moment for me, for sure. It is my academic birthplace. I came home, proud to wear my Aggie ring, able to be an Aggie talking to Aggies, blessed to be among my tribe once again. I'm a first-generation college student from humble beginnings. I'm a three-time Aggie and a three-time dean. I'm one who made it back home.

I wrote earlier about the incredible connection I had in Arkansas with Jim Walton over our fathers. Both of us looked up to our dads as heroes in our lives. Any story about coming home is ultimately going to be a story of connection, and on my return to A&M, I was blessed to be able to connect in a deep way with a special man, Mr. Lowry Mays, who is another proud Aggie, just like me.

Lowry is the man who generously donated $15 million to the business school in 1996 and was honored by having the school named after him. But his giving didn't stop there. During the years of my predecessor, Dr. Jerry Strawser, the Mays family gave another $7 million, and in 2017, while I was dean, the family donated $25 million, the largest single donation in the history of the business school. One of my proudest moments came in 2015 when I was honored with the Lowry and Peggy Mays Eminent Scholar Chair in Business.

Lowry made his fortune in the broadcasting business. He founded San Antonio Broadcasting Company, which later became Clear Channel Communications, one of the biggest, most powerful broadcasting companies in the country. I first met Lowry in an interview. He was on the search committee during my interview process, and our first meeting was by phone. In that original conversation, the story of our connection began to emerge. He told me, "So I noticed that you're a sales guy. Me too!" As we got to know one another better, I told him about my first career as a broadcaster. Our connections led to more conversations, and the conversations led to friendship. Today, I'm honored to call Lowry Mays a very dear friend. In fact, I was able to share a special legacy moment with the Mays family as Lowry's granddaughter graduated from Mays Business School in Spring 2021.

> *Goliath doesn't want me fulfilling my calling of transforming lives just like he didn't want David to fulfill his calling of becoming king.*

Only God could've brought the two of us together. Though we're very different, we share a special full-circle connection. We're both Aggies. We're both in the business of selling. And we both come from a broadcasting background. Coming home is all about coming full circle; it's all about special connections.

GIANTS ON THE ROAD TO SUCCESS

Looking back over my incredible journey, I see one constant presence, and that's the giant Goliath. Did you know that your road to success will be lined with giants, always ready to distract you, disable you, or take you out? You can bet that Goliath doesn't want me fulfilling my calling of transforming lives just like he didn't want David to fulfill his calling of becoming king.

I've had to face huge giants like Fear, Poverty, Intimidation, Underestimation, Doubt, and Death throughout my life. And while I'd like to tell you that there is a way to avoid the giants altogether, that's a pipe dream. You might not like hearing it, but giants are a fact of life. That's why I've written this book: to encourage folks not to run away from giants in fear but to face them bravely and run toward them.

After reading this book, what would you do or say differently to someone facing a Goliath? How could you help someone cope with the death of a loved one?

In the course of my job as a fundraiser, I've been privileged to be able to meet and talk with lots of very successful people, people who are capable of donating millions of dollars. I've been able to share some of my stories with them and listen to theirs. And what do you think was consistent about all of them?

With each story of success comes giants, no exceptions. Jesus said it like this: "In this world you will have trouble. But take heart! I have overcome the world" (John 16:33 NIV). He's telling us that in this life, there's going to be giants, there's going to be some bumps and bruises and battles and bloodshed. But with courage that only comes from God, you can run toward your Goliaths, and you can defeat the giants in your path. But from experience, I can tell you that there's no way you can go through these battles without God. You can't face these giants alone.

Moving back home to A&M was just the right move for us at just the right time, but that didn't mean there would not be any more giants. It wasn't long before the dreaded giant called Death came out for another attack.

> *Legacy is about redemption.*
> *What does that mean to you?*

LOSING NECIA

In June of 2008, we lost my dad. Then in September of 2015, we lost my mom. And as terrible as those events were, both my parents lived long and productive lives. In that sense, it was somewhat easier to let them go. But Death had another blow up his sleeve, a blow I never saw coming.

In July of 2019, our eldest daughter, Necia, passed. I'd lost both my parents, and I thought that pain was terrible. But this experience was infinitely worse. Losing a child is not a natural act. Your child is not supposed to go before you. It's unnatural.

Necia's death came so suddenly, so out of the blue, that I still struggle to make sense out of it. The truth of it is that it makes no sense. I've often found myself thinking, *I'm so glad I believe in Jesus.* I don't even know how I would feel if I didn't believe in Him. I'm holding on to what the Bible says. I'm holding on to what God says.

We planted a tree in Necia's honor in our backyard. To me, nothing speaks of legacy quite like a tree. One man plants a tree, and while he may never get to see the tree fully grown, his children and grandchildren for generations get to enjoy the shade from that tree. I guess one way to make sense of Necia's death is to look at it through the lens of legacy. As painful as Necia's death has been for all of us, there has been redemption. And legacy is all about redemption; it's all about coming full circle.

Since Necia's passing, Fern and I have been much more engaged in her children's lives, the girls, Justice and Jaiden, and her son, Jase, who is living with us now. Every time we go in the backyard and see that tree, we think of Necia, her children think of their momma, and they will be able to show that tree to their kids and tell stories about their mother. Generation to generation, that's what legacy is all about. What kind of legacy do you want to leave?

FIVE SMOOTH STONES

1. How do you feel when someone says, "Just because you can't see the reason for something God is doing in your life doesn't mean there isn't one."? Does hearing this help you? If not, why not?

2. Have you ever found yourself in a situation in which you've got to do your job, but you've got something personal and serious going on at the same time? How did you handle it?

3. How have you coped with the giant called Death? What do you say to others to encourage them during this experience?

4. After reading this book, what would you do or say differently to someone facing a Goliath? How could you help someone cope with the death of a loved one?

5. Legacy is about redemption. What does that mean to you?

14

CONCLUSION: LEAVING A LEGACY

Thought-starter: Why should you run toward the Goliaths in your life?

WHY?

So, now that we've come to the last chapter, I must ask, "Why?" What's it all about anyway? Why live a life of purpose? Why take the time and effort to build a strong foundation or find my rhythm or dare to believe? Why bother?

You've just got to love the skeptics, don't you? I'm a natural skeptic, and I approach almost any new premise with the big question, "Why?" That's part of what has made me successful throughout my career in academia. I'm not just curious; I'm skeptical. So, it's only fair for me to apply that same amount of skepticism to my premise. I say that we should run toward our Goliaths, but the skeptic in me shouts, "Why?"

I have a one-word answer for you: legacy. The act of leaving something important behind for those who are coming along after we're gone. Why is it essential to build a strong foundation? Legacy. Your foundation must be strong enough for the generations coming after you to build upon. Strong foundations are built on solid core values. Remember, the true inheritance from my parents and grandparents wasn't money or things. My true inheritance was the core values they handed down to me.

> **Leave them a legacy of dreaming big dreams!**

Why is it vital for you to find your rhythm and discover your calling? Legacy. Your descendants will discover their identity much easier if you can give them some generational context. Telling them stories about their ancestors reminds them of where they come from, leading them to who they are, which is their identity.

Why is it important for you to dare to believe? Legacy. Just like the lyrics in Fern's song, "Dreams don't have an expiration date." If you want your children and grandchildren to dream big dreams, they're going to need to see you dreaming big dreams, even multi-generational dreams that won't be fulfilled in your lifetime. Leave them a legacy of dreaming big dreams!

THE LEGACY CHAPTER

We know that specific chapters in the Bible deal with particular subjects so well and so completely that the chapter becomes unofficially known by that subject. We know 1 Corinthians 13 as the "Love Chapter" and Hebrews 11 as the "Faith Chapter." Well, I believe that 1 Chronicles 22 could be known as the "Legacy Chapter."

In 1 Chronicles 22, we read about what David spent his time doing in his later years. Was he trying to expand his kingdom? Was he trying to accumulate personal wealth? Was he retired, resigned to sitting on his sofa in his palace all day, living off his reputation as a giant killer? No, he wasn't doing any of those things. In his later years, David's mind had turned from the pursuit of personal success to leaving a legacy for the next generation. David committed what was left of his life to collect building materials so his son, Solomon, could build God's temple. And he didn't do the job halfway, either. He pursued this sacred act like everything else in his life, with passion!

In some of David's final words to his son, he says,

> I have taken great pains to provide for the temple of the Lord a hundred thousand talents of gold, a million talents of silver, quantities of bronze and iron too great to be weighed, and wood and stone. And you may add to them. You have many workers: stonecutters, masons and carpenters, as well as those skilled in every kind of work in gold and silver, bronze and iron—craftsmen beyond number. Now begin the work, and the Lord be with you.
> (1 Chr. 22:14–16 NIV)

In his final years, David was conscious of just one thing: leaving a legacy. He was careful to follow a lesson that his descendant, Jesus Christ, would teach generations later when He said, "From everyone who has been given much, much will be demanded; and from the one who has been entrusted with much, much more will be asked" (Luke 12:48 NIV). David knew that he'd been given much in his lifetime and was fully aware of his obligation, committed to leaving an inheritance for his children.

SCATTERING NOT GATHERING

I'm reminded of Fern's favorite quote from Helen Walton that we mentioned earlier in the book. "It's not what you gather but what you scatter that tells what kind of life you have lived." Legacy isn't about gathering or accumulating. It's not about seeing how much you can get. It's about seeing how much you can give. With legacy, the real question isn't what have you been put on this earth to do; it's what have you been put on this earth to leave behind?

I believe in scattering. I believe in making a legacy—not just something I do but the way I choose to live my life. In my own family, our children have college degrees, and I have descendants who have moved into sales and leadership positions. I'm proud to say that our grandson, Jase, Necia's son, is a college student, an Aggie.

The night that Jase graduated high school, Fern and I sat in the audience. As he crossed the stage, I was witnessing something very special, something familiar and incredibly meaningful. This time, I watched my grandkids, Ean and Rylee, look at the confidence that Jase carried. His sister, Jaiden, watched him graduate too. I thought back to when I watched Jo Ann graduate college when I was ten and the goal that I set. Then I imagined what Ean (12), Jaiden (11), and Rylee (10) were thinking and dreaming. This, too, was a defining moment. Fern and I are fully committed to pouring just as much as we can into our adult children—Tracia, Chris, and Elicia—and their children, our grandchildren—Justice, Jase, Jaiden, Amari, Zani, Elijah, Judah, Ezra, Ean, and Rylee.

In addition to leaving behind a sales institute and a business education complex, I have scattered scholarships and competitive grants across this country. Fern and I endowed a couple of scholarships at A&M for students interested in sales. We also give annually to the National Collegiate Sales Competition for undergraduate students competing to be the top sales students in the country. I'm proud to be a donor to the Ph.D. Project, which is designed to help underrepresented minorities in business join doctoral programs to become professors, a big part of my own story. We also provide a competitive grant annually to doctoral students in the Marketing Doctoral Students Association based on their research productivity and promise. Recently, a group of colleagues and I set up an endowment through the American Marketing Association Foundation to provide competitive grants to sales researchers who make a long-term impact on the field through their research publications.

For Fern and me, leaving a legacy is about going full circle and seeding into the lives of others. It's about scattering our blessings and leaving a foundation for our descendants to build upon, as David did for his son Solomon.

AN OBLIGATION TO LEGACY

As I reflected on this idea of legacy, it occurred to me that it's not just about us. If it were, then the pursuit of success in this life would be our ultimate aim, but it's not. We have an obligation to legacy, which involves preparing the way for those who will come after us, our lineage, our descendants, our kids, and our grandkids. We have a responsibility to sow into their lives, giving them a leg up into their destiny and calling, helping them find their rhythm.

Speaking of descendants, while writing this chapter, I thought we could all benefit by hearing the perspective of my son, Chris. He makes some brilliant legacy points. Here's Chris:

Thanks, Pops! When I think of legacy, four main points come to mind.

1. **Godly people raise up others** by leaving a legacy to those who come after. They're committed to making the lives of their descendants better. Think about the story of Jesus healing the lame young man in Luke 5:17–26. There's no way the man would have even gotten in front of Jesus without the help of his four friends. They not only carried the man across town to the house where Jesus was teaching, but they also pulled their friend up on the roof because of the crowd

and let him down in front of Jesus through a hole they'd made! Legacy is all about raising others up. Sometimes literally!

2. **Jesus Christ is the best example of a legacy left for future generations.** John 3:16 says, "For God so loved the world that he gave his one and only Son, that whoever believes in him shall not perish but have eternal life" (NIV). Because of Christ's work on the cross, all humanity has been granted access to God. There's no greater inheritance than eternal life. Talk about leaving a legacy!

3. **Legacy is all about transforming lives.** If you think about it, the whole Bible is simply a collection of stories about how God's people have continually, by His grace, transformed their lives, built upon the groundwork laid by those who had gone before them.

4. **Finally, legacy is not only about transforming lives; it's about transforming entire generations.** Consider this: even the prostitute Rahab, who experienced the miraculous saving grace of God at Jericho, passed down her love of God to her son Boaz, who passed it on to his son Obed. He then passed it on to his son Jesse, who passed it on to his son David, then to Solomon, and so on down the family line, all the way to Jesus, even continuing down to us. We are the legacy of Christ! That's the power of legacy.

Amen, son! What a great way to describe this whole idea of the power of legacy. Legacy is a powerful weapon in our hands when we run toward the giants such as Death, Doubt, Fear, Insignificance, Poverty, Regret, and Underestimation.

CONCLUSION: LEAVING A LEGACY

A GREAT CLOUD OF WITNESSES

Hebrews 12:1 says, "Therefore, since we are surrounded by such a great cloud of witnesses, let us throw off everything that hinders and the sin that so easily entangles. And let us run with perseverance the race marked out for us" (NIV). Not only does legacy require a responsibility to those who come after us, but it also requires a responsibility to those who have gone before us.

> *Have you ever thanked God for the legacy of your ancestors?*

Have you ever thanked God for the legacy of your ancestors? No matter who you are or what you've accomplished in your life, *you haven't achieved success all on your own.* You've succeeded by standing on the shoulders of those who have gone before. Believe me, even as I write this book (which is a legacy piece in itself), I'm keenly aware of my grandparents, my parents, and my oldest daughter Necia, who have all gone before me and are a living part of my "cloud of witnesses." They're watching to see how I'm investing in the legacy they left to me.

IT'S NEVER TOO LATE TO LEAVE A LEGACY

No matter who you are or what you've done, or what you haven't done, you need to know that it's never too late to leave a legacy. You might have been sucker-punched by the giant called Regret, but it's not too late. You might have been scared to death by the giant called Fear, but it's not too late. You might have been beaten down by the giant called Self-Pity, but it's not too late. You might have been deeply wounded by the giant called Insignificance, but it's not too late. The fact is, no matter what giants you are facing, it's never too late because of the legacy left to you by Jesus Christ. My prayer for you is that you would discover His saving grace for yourself and begin to live a life worthy of His supreme sacrifice.

You may not live to see your dreams come true, but your children will, your grandchildren will, those whose lives you've been pouring into will see the fruit of those dreams. That's His promise to each of us. Deuteronomy 7:9 says, "Know therefore that the Lord your God is God; he is the faithful God, keeping his covenant of love to a thousand generations of those who love him and keep his commandments" (NIV).

God said it. You can believe it. Now, go! Build on your foundation. Find your rhythm. Dare to believe. It's time for you to pick up your sling and run toward your Goliaths!

"FIGHT"
Fern Walker Jones

The darkness cannot stand the light
Walk in God's LOVE
And in the Power of His Might

In the darkness we cannot see
Turn on the light to slay the enemy

The world may be broken
But God has spoken ... through me

He said, get on your knees ... and FIGHT
He arms us with His Word ... so FIGHT
Against those things we cannot see ... just FIGHT
Stand firm in His truth ... and FIGHT

God has given us authority
Over ALL the power of the enemy
That came to destroy you and me
But God came to give us life abundantly

In Him we have peace
And can live in harmony

Get on your knees ... and FIGHT
He arms us with His Word ... so FIGHT
Against the things we cannot see ... just FIGHT
Stand firm in His truth ... and FIGHT

Lift your hands and FIGHT
The Word of God FOREVER stands ... so FIGHT
Sing praises to the Lord ... just FIGHT
The good fight of faith ... just FIGHT

RUN TOWARD YOUR GOLIATHS

Not by (our) power
Not by (our) might
But by His Spirit we have won this Fight
NOT by (our) power
NOT by (our) might
But by HIS SPIRIT we have won this FIGHT

Oh Yeah, Oh Yeah!!!

Get on your knees ... and FIGHT
He arms us with His Word ... so FIGHT
Against those things we cannot see ... just FIGHT
Stand firm in His truth ... and FIGHT

Lift your hands and FIGHT
The Word of God FOREVER stands ... so FIGHT
Sing praises to the Lord ... so FIGHT
The good fight of faith ... Oh FIGHT

Fight! Oh, Fight ... just FIGHT!
Fight! Oh, Fight ... just FIGHT!

This war is NOT against mankind
We fight against broken hearts and the Evil in Our
    Minds
So, Fight ... just Fight.

Get on your knees and Fight!
Lift your hands and Fight!
Put on the armor of God *and Fight!*

CONCLUSION: LEAVING A LEGACY

ACKNOWLEDGMENTS

To our adult children, grandchildren, and great-grandchildren to come, Mema and I love you deeply. Always remember who you are and *whose* you are. You come from a long line of entrepreneurs who walked by faith, worked hard, and God made a way when it seemed there was no way. May God bless you greatly. Be blessed and be a blessing. Mema and I will be cheering you on. – Papa

Thank you to the family and friends who read drafts of this book and provided feedback and suggestions. I acknowledge the following (in alphabetical order by last name).

Jo Ann Jones Burbridge
Paul Busch
Fern Jones
Mike Jones
John Mason
Diane McDonald
Janet Parish
Bill Peel
Joan Quintana
Mike Staires
Tyson Voelkel
Holland Webb